A Corner of North Oxford

The Community at the Crossroads

Catherine Robinson
and Liz Wade

Graffiti Press
Oxford

Published by Graffiti Press
28 Polstead Road, Oxford, OX2 6TN

First published in 2010
Second impression 2012

ISBN 978-0-9566333-1-6

Sales of the first print run of this book supported the renovation
of the war memorial in St Margaret's Parish, North Oxford.
All profits from the second impression will be given to
The Gatehouse, a charity based at St Giles' Church in Oxford offering
food, shelter, and company to homeless and poorly housed people.

Typeset by Oxford Designers and Illustrators, Aristotle Lane, Oxford

Printed and bound in the United Kingdom by
Lightning Source, Milton Keynes

Contents

Preface

WE HAVE WRITTEN this book to raise money for the restoration of the parish War Memorial, which was erected on the corner of St Margaret's Road and Kingston Road in 1919 to honour the 47 men from our community who fell in the Great War.

The Memorial, a late flowering of the Victorian Gothic Revival, has not worn well. Those who designed it and paid for it must have known that it was fragile, but must also have been confident that future generations would look after it. They did not know, as they gathered for the dedication on St Margaret's Day in 1920, that their war would not be "the War to end all Wars" and that, nearly one hundred years later, our community would be very different from theirs.

So we found ourselves asking: Is there a community here now? If so, what makes it one? If there is a community, why would it want to spend its money on rebuilding a memorial that a few people love, a few people loathe, and most people are indifferent to? We have had some thoughts on these questions, but we expect that, in this articulate, contentious parish of St Margaret's, people will have their own answers.

Our thinking is this: a community becomes dysfunctional and ceases to exist if it has no meeting places. We are fortunate in this corner of North Oxford to have a community centre – St Margaret's Institute in Polstead Road – which was nearly lost to us at the turn of the millennium. At the eleventh hour, the community realised that, if it did not pull together, the building where we and our predecessors had learned, played, argued, and celebrated for more than a century would vanish. The experience knitted us together in a way that we could not have expected, and the results continue to enrich our community.

But the community is more than the Institute: it's The Anchor pub next door, and Aladdin Garage and Bunter's Deli round the corner. They form the hub around which the community manages its everyday life. Farther afield, but still within St Margaret's Parish, are the Church and the Primary School of St Philip & St James, where for a hundred years local children have been educated – recently moved from one end of the parish to the other, but in essence unchanged. We also have the canal and precious green places: the recreation ground, Port Meadow, and – the jewel in our parish crown – the Trap Grounds, saved in our generation, so that on a warm July night you can see glow worms, just as our predecessors did a hundred years ago.

However, even if you agree that we have the building blocks in place for a community, do we actually still have one? There is evidence that we do: the young mums having coffee at The Anchor on a Friday morning; the crowded noticeboard outside Bunter's; the Aristotle playground teeming with toddlers; the annual May Morning gathering at the crossroads; parties at the Institute where you have to shout to make yourself heard above the drum beat of the disco.

But, even if there is a community, why should it spend its money rebuilding a war memorial? Maybe because, as a part of this community's baggage, we have inherited these 47 men. Keeping their memory alive is a responsibility that falls to us all – we are their family now. It doesn't seem to matter whether the War Memorial upsets our aesthetics, or whether war itself upsets our moral sense: the important thing is that the Memorial recognises 47 ordinary men who did something extraordinary for their community, and for their world – which is now ours.

The Old Hatchet Inn, c.1906

1 The Community at the Crossroads

THIS BOOK TELLS the story of a community which began to develop 150 years ago about a mile from the centre of Oxford, in a corner of a suburb which had been steadily spreading beyond the city walls since the middle of the nineteenth century.

As small businesses in the city centre were crowded out by the expansion of the University, their proprietors and employees found modest new homes and premises to the north in Walton Street and Kingston Road. At the same time, the families of academics, clergymen, and retired civil servants of the Empire were establishing themselves in the neo-gothic splendour of villas in Banbury Road and Woodstock Road, and the leafy connecting streets. The families of labourers who built the villas, or toiled at Lucy's Iron Foundry, or unloaded coal on the canal wharf found decent, affordable homes in Hayfield Road. At the heart of the community were the newly built church of St Margaret, the Working Men's Institute in Polstead Road, the school of St Philip & St James in Leckford Road, the shops and stables in Hayfield Road – and Dolley's Hut, the ancient hostelry which preceded The Anchor Inn as we know it today. Even before local residents were united in grief over the loss of many young lives in the First World War – lives that are commemorated on the war memorial outside the church – this neighbourhood had developed into a remarkably close-knit community, as we hope to show in the chapters that follow.

Early days

THE EARLIEST EVIDENCE of human settlement in the area dates back 4,000 years. Implements from the Bronze Age (c. 2000–1500 BCE) have been found in Aristotle Lane, and early Bronze Age pots were found in graves excavated in Polstead Road. On Port Meadow, near the ditch alongside Burgess Field, there are signs of six "ring ditches", probably funeral barrows. One of them, known as Round Hill, was excavated in 1842 by Sheriff Hunt, and later by T. E. Lawrence ("Lawrence of Arabia"), when he was a schoolboy living in Polstead Road. We have no record of what, if anything, they found.

Some time during the middle Iron Age (about 350 to 50 BCE), three small farmsteads were established, with several paddocks for livestock, due west of the Bronze Age sites. The evidence can be seen from the air in dry summers, when the boundaries of the prehistoric sites show up as a darker green than the surrounding land.

The Romans were here too: evidence of a settlement has been found in Chalfont Road and Polstead Road, and just west of St Margaret's Church. But nothing is known of the area in the Dark Ages, and we have to fast-forward to the Middle Ages to see the first traces of the landscape that is familiar to us today.

Aristotle Lane

ARISTOTLE LANE IS an ancient right of way, known originally as "the Lower Way to Wolvercote". Until 1841, when a bridge was built over the canal nearer to the city at Walton Well Lane, Aristotle Lane was the chief entrance to Port Meadow from the east. Its use was much disputed in the Middle Ages by the city authorities and the abbesses of Godstow Nunnery, who owned land hereabouts. Eventually, to keep an eye on the lane and prevent its being blocked, the city council built a house at the eastern end to accommodate "the reeve's man" (a reeve was a kind of feudal estate manager). The *Victoria County History* records the presence of a herdsman's house at the gate to

2

the Lane in 1582; it was used in 1603 and 1608 as a "pest house" to isolate victims of the plague, and it finally fell into ruin in 1629.

The most dramatic incident in the history of our neighbourhood occurred on 3 June 1644, when King Charles I escaped the siege of Oxford. He marched north by night with 5,000 men along the line of what is now Kingston Road, under the shadow of the tree-crowned gravel bank which in those days ran along its length. They escaped along Aristotle Lane, to cross Port Meadow, ford the Thames, and make a dash for the West Country.

It was over Aristotle Bridge between 1849 and 1852 that thousands of tons of gravel were taken by tramway from Cabbage Hill (later to become Kingston Road) and Lark Hill (later to become Chalfont Road). The gravel was used for the construction of the Great Western Railway, 200 yards to the west. According to the antiquarian writer Henry Minn, the gravel bank had been so high that a door at the back of the old Anchor Inn "now opening from one of the upper rooms, had at one time been at ground level". Today the only surviving remnant of the bank forms the western boundary of St Margaret's churchyard in Kingston Road. The removal of the gravel bank and terrace cleared the way for the eventual development of this area of North Oxford.

"Paraffin Liz"

PARAFFIN LIZ WAS one of the local eccentrics for whom respectable society once allowed more space than it does nowadays. In the 1930s she lived in a shed in Aristotle Lane near the railway crossing. Her real name was Miss Dearing, and she was reputed to have been a former Librarian of Somerville College. Eventually she was reduced to making a living by giving riding lessons to children on Port Meadow (using horses that did not belong to her). According to local legend, "She always rode bare-back. She was a queer old soul, as skinny as a herring. She wore men's boots, and string for a belt, and her niece paid for her to have dinner in the Randolph Hotel every night."

The Henfold Road, with Navigation House on the left, 1900

2 A Public House: The Anchor

Aristotle's Well

OUR STORY REALLY begins with a well, situated in what is now the cellar of number 90 Kingston Road, almost on the corner of Kingston Road and Aristotle Lane. Anthony Wood, writing in 1667, noted that this well "was anciently called Brumman's Well, together with that at Walton, because Brumman le Rich, or de Walton [one of the knights of Robert d'Oilly, the Norman governor of Oxford Castle] lived and owned lands about the said wells".

According to Wood: "After his time, if not likely before, it was christened by the name of Aristotle's Well, because it was then (as now it is) frequented in the summer season by our peripatetics". So the well was a favourite haunt of scholars, walking out from Oxford through the fields, presumably discussing philosophy (and starting, perhaps, from Plato's Well at the southern end of what is now Walton Street). In 1718 Thomas Hearne recorded in his Journal that there was a "house of refreshment" near Aristotle's Well, and it is tempting to suppose that he meant a cottage on the site of the present Anchor Inn which appears on Benjamin Cole's map of Port Meadow, produced in 1720. Cole called the cottage "Heathfields Hutt", but he seems to have mistaken the name, for we know that a man named William Heyfield lived there around that time. *Jackson's Oxford Journal* announced on January 24 1778: "On Tuesday last died, aged upwards of 90, Mr Heyfield, who for many years kept the Hutt known by his name in the Road leading from the City to Port Meadow."

Heyfield's Hutt ... Dolley's Hut ... what's in a name?

THE ANCHOR INN as we know it today, standing at the crossroads formed by Aristotle Lane, Hayfield Road, Polstead Road, and Kingston Road, dates from 1937 and bears no resemblance to the original hostelry on the site, known in the 18th century as Heyfield's Hutt, and in the 19th as Dolley's Hut.

In the years when William Heyfield presided over it – from 1721, if not earlier, until some time before his death in 1778 – the inn seems to have had a rather dubious reputation. We learn from *Jackson's Oxford Journal* (25 February 1764) of a game of cards there in which the eminent Dr Webb, a tooth-drawer, blood-letter, and wig-maker, lost 44 guineas and the mortgage deeds of two houses in the parish of St Thomas. There is a hint that the doctor may have been the victim of a gang of card-sharps. Never the most reputable of public houses in the old days, it was frequented in the 19th century, according to Henry Minn, by undergraduates who brought their dogs for the purposes of rat-coursing on Port Meadow – "a bag of rats being supplied by local waterside loafers".

The Hut was acquired by Hall's Oxford Brewery in 1796. By 1845 it appears as "The Anchor" in Hunt's City of Oxford Directory, which named the landlord as Anthony Harris. Longevity seems to have been the hallmark of the Anchor landlords: Harris took over the licence in 1796 and died 51 years later, still presiding over the bar, in 1847. In 1852 William Dolley (son of Thomas Dolley, a brewer and publican at the Dolphin & Anchor in St Aldates) moved in with his wife Charlotte and ran the inn for a quarter of a century until 1877. The establishment acquired the affectionate nickname "Dolley's Hut", by which it was known until quite recently, even though it was demolished and rebuilt by Hall's in 1936/37. Older residents of Hayfield Road, interviewed by the author in 1993, remembered the original inn as a cosy and cheerful place, with small poky rooms and low ceilings ("just like a dolly's hut", remarked one man).

William Dolley must have been a notable character, because his name also became attached to Aristotle's Well, which was known in the nineteenth century as the Wishing Well, or Dolley's Well, until it was bricked up in 1889.

"Shake them bobbins!"

THE PUB WAS always a favourite with canal-boat families, and it is pleasant to think of Alfred Hone senior, a veteran of the Oxford Canal, singing in the snug in the 1890s: "He could play the squeezebox, and dance and sing, all at the same time. He had a clear true whistle too, and a rattle of wooden bobbins. 'Shake them bobbins!' he used to sing. It was a song the old boat-chaps used to sing to make their horses get a move on." (This recollection of Alfred Hone was recorded by Sheila Stewart in her book *Ramlin Rose: The Boatwoman's Story*.)

The Anchor has been through many changes since those days. After it was rebuilt, it reopened in June 1937 under the tenancy of Mr P. Jones and his wife. Since 2006 the pub has been owned and run by head chef Jamie King and his wife Charlotte, the front-of-house manager. It was credited by *The Good Food Guide 2010* with serving "the best pub food in Oxford", and it hosts monthly meetings of the Anchor Book Club (to which the author of the book in question is usually invited!). But it still serves real ales, and locals can gather in the bar to watch football and rugby matches on TV. And it continues the tradition of serving breakfast and beer at 6 am every May Morning, when Morris Men from Headington Quarry and Eynsham dance at the crossroads, under the watchful eye of Michael Black's life-size plaster Ox, garlanded with May blossom. When you see the ox being trundled down Woodstock Road in the dusk of the previous evening from its quarters at Wytham Abbey, you know that summer is indeed i-comen in.

Hayfield wharf, Oxford Canal, c. 1890. Note the pair of coal boats, crewed by one man and five women

3 A Canal and a Railway

Hayfield's Hut wharf

THE OXFORD CANAL, built to bring coal from Warwickshire collieries, reached Banbury in 1778 and the wharf at Hayfield's Hut in May 1789. Coal merchants travelled long distances with horse-drawn carts to take deliveries from the wharf. Trade was so brisk that within six months of the opening of the wharf the minute book of the Oxford Canal Company recorded an instruction to the Company's contractors to "repair forthwith the Carriage Road [Rackham's Lane, now St Margaret's Road] from the Turnpike Road [Woodstock Road] to Hayfield Hutt".

Besides serving as a distribution point for coal (and probably other heavy goods such as slate, salt, and road-stone), the wharf in Hayfield's Hut Lane was the site of considerable industrial activity. When St John's College (which had been buying up canal-side land since the turn of the century) advertised a lease on the wharf to interested parties in 1839, the notice (now preserved in the Bodleian Library) listed the following features, in addition to a dwelling house and four tenements: a covered dock for boat-building, workshops, sheds, and kilns for the making of bricks, lime, and tiles. At least one brick kiln survived until 1866. The wharf was provided with stables for the boatmen's horses and mules and, later, with a weighing office. Other stables were available on the south side of Aristotle Bridge in the yard on the corner of Kingston Road. A boathouse erected there in 1790 harboured the Canal Company's own boat.

On Hayfield's Hut wharf in the 1870s there was a Mission Room, which was supported by the congregation of the church of St Philip & St James in Woodstock Road. Sunday afternoon services were held here for the benefit of the boatpeople (for whose welfare and morals there was much concern in Victorian society). The Women's Guild of the church paid half the rent, and several of the men from this prosperous, philanthropic congregation taught at a night school held there during the winter months. The Mission Room was pulled down in 1883.

Some time around 1875, a tall brick building called Navigation House was built on the wharf. Here lived Thomas Johnson, described in the Oxford Directory as a "coal and manure merchant and beer retailer". He was assisted by his son-in-law, Anthony Harris (son of the landlord of The Anchor on the opposite side of the road). On wash-days in the 1920s, Mrs Mary Harris, wife of Albert Harris, the foreman on the wharf, would cook faggots and peas on her kitchen range, and the women of Hayfield Road would send their children down the street with basins to fetch dinner for the family. Local boys could earn a few pence by helping to groom and feed the boatmen's horses after school. The wharf closed down in the early 1950s, but Navigation House lingered on until the 1960s, when it was demolished to make way for the offices of Midland Builders (now occupied by Oxford Designers & Illustrators).

A familiar feature of the wharf in our own times is the narrowboat *The Venturer*, moored here when it is not cruising on the waterways with parties of disabled people, elderly people, or children and young people with special needs. Seventy feet long and specially designed to accommodate wheelchairs, *The Venturer* was launched in 1988 by the Prince of Wales. The scheme is managed by the Oxfordshire Narrowboat Trust and run entirely by volunteers.

The boat people

THE LATE MRS Doris Thicke, a long-time resident of Hayfield Road, recalled in 1993:

> *The canal people were very friendly. The same families would travel up and down the canal all year. I remember the Skinners and the Beauchamps. They all waved when they passed the end of our garden. The men used to throw their boots into the garden of number 3, for Tommy Tombs to mend them. They would collect them on the way back up. The boats had glistening brasses, and clothes hung out to dry, as white as milk. Those women were tough! They wore hob-nailed boots, and unloaded coal just like the men. But they put on clean aprons and caps to visit Dolly's Hut. They couldn't read or write: they just signed with a cross.*

Jack and Rose Skinner regularly delivered coal from collieries near Coventry to Hayfield Wharf and "the Radiators" factory to the north (now part of the Waterways estate). In the 1940s, Barlow's, the carrying company, paid them 3 shillings and 9 pence per ton, which amounted to about £6 for a full load. The round trip took two weeks, and they were not paid for the week in which they returned empty. (Jack: *"It was a hard life. We used to work 16 or 17 hours a day, six or seven days a week. Many's the time me and her have set off before dawn and finished in the dark."* ... Rose: *"We used to eat as we went along – and I used to cook as we went along an' all! Cooking with one hand and steering with the other. And the little ones* [they had four children] *playing in the empty hold, or tied to the chimney when we were loaded. You needed eyes in the back of your head."*) Although coal was their staple cargo, the Skinners also carried timber, tar, and corned beef.

By the mid-1950s the canal, which had been losing trade to the road haulage business since the war, was no longer being dredged every Whit Monday and was silting up and becoming choked with weeds. There was talk of closing it. Public opposition to the closure was demonstrated at a protest meeting held in Oxford Town Hall on 3 June 1955, chaired by none other than the poet John Betjeman. By this time, Jack and Rose were working for Willow Wren, a small independent carrying company formed in 1953 with some surplus boats bought from British Waterways. Jack recalls the epic journey that he and Rose undertook in 1954 on their boat *Redshank*, towing the butty boat *Greenshank*, to prove that the canal was still navigable:

> *Me and her and Willow Wren put our heads together and decided the best way to save the canal was to prove that it could still carry traffic. So we brought 50 tons of coal from Nuneaton to Juxon's wharf for Morrell's Brewery. We did all right till we got to Dolly's Hut. The water there was very shallow, because the kids had thrown rubbish into it. We had to bowhaul the butty through* [drag it along with a rope from the towpath], *but we did it!*

The missing bridge

SHARP-EYED WALKERS ALONG the towpath will notice that Aristotle Bridge is numbered 240, and the next bridge south, at Walton Well Road, is number 242. What happened to 241? It is there in the report of the Chain Survey undertaken by the Oxford Canal Company in 1840 (which recorded every bridge, lock, and other notable structure along the 90-mile length of the canal). Ten chains (one-eighth of a mile) from "Hayfields Hut Bridge" was "the Workhouse Bridge": just south of where the builder's yard of Hutchins and Green in Southmoor Road now fronts the canal on the east bank. A photograph taken in 1868 shows it as a timber drawbridge, similar in design to the bridge near St Edward's School. The 1876 Ordnance Survey map shows it clearly, but it was demolished by 1882, when the houses at the north end of Southmoor Road began to be built.

The name "Workhouse Bridge" links it with the City Workhouse, established on Rats and Mice Hill (now Wellington Square) in 1771. According to the *Victoria County History*, for many years until 1865 the Oxford Board of Guardians, responsible for the welfare of the workhouse inmates, managed a small mixed farm on the banks of the canal, on land known as Pepper Hills. A map of 1846 commissioned by the London, Oxford, and Cheltenham Railway shows "Pepper Hill" on the west bank, and "Further Pepper Hill" on the east bank, where now the gardens of Southmoor Road slope down to the water. Linking them was Bridge 241, "the Workhouse Bridge". This area was sufficiently isolated from the city for a cholera hospital and dispensary to be erected on Further Pepper Hill, after the Radcliffe Infirmary refused to admit victims during the terrible 22-week epidemic of 1832. The location was somewhat ironic, given the popular belief at the time that cholera was spread from town to town by canal boats and their crews. According to Henry Minn, the cholera hospital was later dismantled and re-erected on the west side of Woodstock Road, to serve as an isolation hospital for victims of smallpox; indeed, the Ordnance Survey map of 1876 shows a "Pest House" standing in orchards on land between Polstead and Frenchay roads.

Otters and bitterns

UNTIL THE 1950S the canal was clean enough for local children to swim in, and Mrs Jessie Harding, born in 1910 and resident in Hayfield Road all her life, remembered in her ninetieth year: *"You could see the bottom from the drawbridge to Aristotle Lane, and it was full of roach and perch. We used to fish for 'red soldiers' [perch?] with a bent pin and a bit of string."* In the 1990s Ralph Coates, recalling his childhood 80 years previously, remembered that corncrakes could be heard calling in the field north of Aristotle Lane. Mrs Sylvia Johnson, who was born in Kingston Road in 1908 and lived there for 93 years, remembered this stretch of the canal as far more rural than it is now: *"There was much more wildlife in the old days – water voles, grass-snakes, and dab-chicks. I saw an otter in the Isis from Port Meadow once, and you could hear bitterns by the river.*" Mrs Johnson, interviewed by the author in 1999, recalled that the canal seemed to freeze more often in the old days. She remembered skating to work in the town centre, and the arrival of the iron boat drawn by six horses, carrying eight men on each side, rocking the boat from side to side to break the ice.

Trains and trams

FROM THE END of the 18th century, trade thrived on the canal for at least 100 years, despite competition from the railways. The line from Didcot to Oxford was opened in 1844; in 1850 a line was built to Banbury and extended northwards to Warwick and Birmingham in 1853. In January 1907 Port Meadow Halt was opened on the northern side of the bridge (known as Old Man's Bridge) at Aristotle Lane. The passenger fare from here to Wolvercote was one penny, and the journey to Oxford station cost two pence. No trace of the halt now remains, except the crossing to the allotments. It served the old LNWR line to Bletchley but seems to have been uneconomical, for it was closed in 1926. Ralph Coates recalled that at some point in the 1930s a Mr Hinson was run over by a train on the crossing, and both his legs were severed. He was found the following morning, still alive, by a person walking a dog – and was eventually able to return to work as a proof-reader at Oxford University Press.

To complete this brief history of local transport systems, we should note that in 1881 the Oxford Tramway Company was established. Horse-drawn trams brought passengers up Walton Street as far as Leckford Road. In 1914 they were replaced by buses with open-top decks and external staircases. The number 3 came up to St Margaret's Road. In the 1980s the mini-bus service began, and it has proved to be a boon (if only once an hour) to the community ever since.

4 A Parish Church: St Margaret's

"A pearl of great price"

IN 1875 A mission room was established in an old skin shed on the canal wharf in Hayfield Road, mainly to meet the needs of the boat people of North Oxford, whose welfare and morals greatly exercised polite Victorian society. Another example of this philanthropic concern was the boatmen's floating chapel, moored in Jericho.

The mission room was replaced in 1883 by the brand-new St Margaret's Church, on the corner of Kingston Road and St Margaret's Road: a substantial but rather stolid building, designed by H. G. W. Drinkwater in decorated Gothic style to reflect the sympathies of what was then a High Church congregation. The date on the bell, 1876, indicates that it was taken from the mission room and installed at St Margaret's. Drinkwater had a considerable reputation at the time for designing and restoring Anglican churches in Gothic revival style, but also for designing pubs: the Cape of Good Hope on the Plain and the Brewery Gate in St Thomas' Street are his. When it was built, the church was designed to hold a congregation of 400.

Two other major architects associated with the Arts and Crafts movement were involved: G. F. Bodley and Cecil Hare were responsible for introducing much of the fine joinery and carving within the church. Bodley designed the pulpit, the rood-screen, the rood, and the base of the tower. The tower was never completed, because diocesan funds for church building were diverted from St Margaret's to create the new church of St Andrew's in Linton Road in 1906.

Cecil Hare designed St Margaret's Puginesque reredos, aumbry, baptistery screen, and font, and also the reredos of the All Souls side chapel. There are two treasures in this church: the aumbry (a spectacular Pre-Raphaelite wall-chest) and the stained glass in the three windows of the Lady Chapel at the eastern end of the south aisle, designed by another highly respected architect, F. C. Eden. These have recently been restored, because the heat of the sun had caused them to become mis-shapen.

Most poignantly, on the western end of the south aisle Eden designed a window to commemorate the death of two brothers in the Great War, John and Charles Bridson. For the face of St Alban, it would appear that the stained-glass artist has used a photograph of John Bridson.

Window commemorating Second Lieutenant John Bridson

The foundation stone, laid in 1883, was inscribed with the words "Una pretiosa margarita" ("a pearl of great price"). Under it was placed a bottle containing, rather unimaginatively, copies of the *Gospeller* and the *Morning Post*, an Order of Service, and some newly minted silver coins.

St Margaret's relationship with the church of St Philip and St James fluctuated like that between a parent and a child. This dynamic was symbolised from the start in the decision to lay St Margaret's foundation stone on the twenty-first birthday of Phil & Jim, when the hope was expressed that "mother and daughter would do well" (Dr Gray, first vicar of the parish). Initially St Margaret's was a daughter church to Phil &Jim; it became independent as a successful young church in 1896; but was reunited with the original mother church, older and wiser by now, in 1976. Then, three years after the closure of Phil & Jim in 1982, St Margaret was to find a congenial partner in St Giles.

The church and the wider community

SINCE 1997 ST MARGARET'S vicar has been Andrew Bunch, who has moved the church and the wider parish on in ways that most of his predecessors would not have recognised. The annual round of services and festivals continues, but it is complemented by a number of innovative projects, ranging from a millennium drama starring St Margaret and her dragon to large-scale concerts featuring the church's newly re-configured organ. Recently the church has been in the forefront of a "Green Shoots" initiative, aiming to present to all local residents practical and imaginative ways of coming to grips with the consequences of climate change. A series of initiatives and building projects has made the church building more accessible and useful to the church and the local community. In these various ways there has been a sustained drive to integrate the life of the church with that of the surrounding community, which otherwise might not have much connection with the worshipping life of the church.

The music of St Margaret's is one of the glories of this church. On St Margaret's Festival Sunday in July 2010, the choir of 40 singers gave a first performance of a Mass composed by local composer Gabriel Jackson in memory of Dr Gwyneth Davey. An extraordinarily beautiful occasion, created out of the talent and commitment of many people, it was a high point for the very proficient choir, which Sunday by Sunday enriches worship in the church.

Like any parish church, St Margaret's depends on individuals both within and associated with the congregation to give it personality and driving force. But it is luckier than many churches in the energy and quality of talents that so many people give to it. Members of the wider parish are vital too; they come for the great events in their lives, and to mark the passing of those  who are important to the life of our community. For instance, the funeral of Nicholas Vernicos in 2003 was a major event, when more than four hundred of us somehow packed into the church to show our affection for Nicholas and his family. For years they had graciously managed Bunter's Deli as a corner shop, social service, and information centre for our community, and at Nicholas' funeral we wanted to pay tribute to his generosity, and that of this family.

The church has always provided a place where these moments in our community life can find a dignified expression, but these days St Margaret's tries to move outside its established role and to meet its parishioners' needs in imaginative and sometimes unexpected ways. It seeks to affirm the community in all that enriches our vision of life in the past, present, and future.

5 A Community Centre: St Margaret's Institute

PART 1: AT THE HEART OF THE COMMUNITY

The working men's club

ST MARGARET'S INSTITUTE OWES its foundation to a typically Victorian blend of philanthropy and self-help. It was built in Polstead Road, north Oxford, on the initiative of some well-to-do members of the congregation of St Philip & St James. These public-spirited parishioners raised subscriptions for the building of a Working Men's Institute, "to provide rational amusement and instruction for working men of any creed, sect, or opinions, who may thus be kept out of public houses" – according to a letter from one local gentleman to another, soliciting a contribution in August 1889. He added: "The working men are taking it up and raising money themselves."

Presumably the landlord of The Anchor Inn next door to the proposed Institute did not subscribe to the cause! The working men in question, who would have been the pub's regular customers, lived round the corner in the terraced cottages of Kingston Road, and in the newly built terraces of "artisans' dwellings" in Hayfield Road. They worked at Lucy's Iron Foundry or the Oxford University Press, on the railway or the coal yard on the nearby canal wharf, or as seasonal labourers on building sites.

In raising money for a working men's club, the middle-class parishioners of St Philip & St James church in Woodstock Road were continuing a tradition of philanthropy that had begun in 1875 with the establishment of a Mission Room on the wharf opposite The Anchor. The women members of the church had paid half the rent of the premises, and several of the men served as volunteer teachers at a small night school held at the Mission during the winter months. The Mission Room was demolished in  1883, perhaps in response to the opening of St Margaret's Church (the daughter church of "Phil and Jim") in the same year; some of its social and educational functions were taken over by the Working Men's Institute, which opened in 1890.

Enough money was raised by public subscription to buy from St John's College the 99-year lease of a plot of land on which to build a three-storey parish institute (the first building to be erected in Polstead Road). The architect was H.G.W. Drinkwater, who also designed St Margaret's Church (opened 1883,  finished 1893) and the parish school in Leckford Road. The dedication stone of the Institute was laid on 8 May 1883, and the building (originally named "The St Philip & St. James Working Men's Institute") finally opened in 1890. On the ground floor was a large room for boys, with its own separate entrance to the left of the front door. There were two rooms for men on the first floor, a flat in the attic, and lavatories in the cellar. Within five years the Institute had become so successful that an appeal was launched to extend it. The appeal leaflet read plaintively:

> Music, Dancing, Boxing, and Gymnastics … Concerts and Dinners have frequently been held, but with great inconvenience … the space is limited and the ventilation insufficient … readers find it

impossible to obtain quiet where games are played, and ... by the loss of some of its oldest and best members the Club has suffered considerably ...

The target of the appeal was £800, which was duly donated, and by 1895 the Institute had been doubled in size with the creation of a committee room on the ground floor and, next to the billiards room on the first floor, a spacious games room for cards, darts, chess, and dominoes. Off this was a washroom and  bathroom (a boon to the working men whose houses had been built without baths). The billiards room was said to be the finest of its kind in Oxford, with raised cushioned seating round the table. The Oxford Billiards League held its championship matches here. The library contained all kinds of books and numerous periodicals. In every room there was a blazing coal fire. Everything was of good quality: real silver cutlery and real china. The Club, which was open from 2 pm each day, was a flourishing concern. It usually numbered about 150 members, who had to apply for admission and be sponsored. But history does not record whether it succeeded in its initial aim of keeping working men and boys out of public houses.

Magic lanterns and Sunday School treats

IN ANY CASE, the Institute was soon serving the whole community, and in particular functioning as a hall for St Margaret's Church; perhaps inevitably, it became known as "St Margaret's Institute" – the name that it still bears today. The early parish magazines are full of accounts of Penny Readings, Lantern Lectures, Sunday School treats, and Missionary Pageants. There was a  Girls' Happy Hour at the turn of the century, when the members made rugs and toy theatres. A short-lived Literary and Scientific Society heard lectures on subjects such as "Italian Masters in the National Gallery". Far more enduring was the St Margaret's Horticultural Society, which organised social events as well as grand shows: in 1902, for instance, a Concert and Dance, to the accompaniment of a Banjo and Mandolin Band. An insight into the close-knit life of this community is given by a poignant entry in the parish magazine in 1901. Referring to the recent terrible loss of HMS Cobra with all hands on board, it mourns the drowning of 23-year-old Leonard Tuffrey of Hayfield Road – *"present at our recent Flower Show"*.

The parish magazines of 1906 give a lively picture of community life in the years before the First World War. The issue for January records:

> On January 3rd the Sunday School assembled at the Institute and found everything prepared for a happy evening. The tea left nothing to be desired; but there was more to follow. In the smaller room a Christmas Tree of large proportions was brilliant with presents and lighted candles, and there was much excitement when the fruits of this Tree were distributed. The children then returned to the larger room, to find that a transformation had taken place: the tables had been removed and a Magic Lantern was ready to commence a varied entertainment under the management of Mr Hallam. The evening closed with a distribution of cake and oranges as the children left the Institute. We are indebted to Miss J. Green and the teachers of the Sunday School for their hard work to secure the great success of the entertainment, and to several friends whose contributions made it possible to give so much pleasure to our children.

In the same month, "the Girls' Guild enjoyed a Tea and a delightful Magic Lantern display, with splendid views of Alpine scenery ... the Boys' Guild and Choir Boys had their Christmas Treat: an evening of

games and refreshments ...the younger members
of the Band of Hope gave an entertainment to
a large audience ... the Men's Guild discussed
'Disestablishment' and 'Religious Education in
Public Elementary Schools' ... and Sir William
Herschel conducted Men's Bible Conferences on
Sundays."

In April 1906, the church magazine recorded "addresses to men
on social subjects on Friday evenings: by the Rev. John Carter of
Pusey House on 'The Problem of the Unemployed' ... by the Rev. A. J.
Carlyle on 'The Church and the Labour Party' ... and by Rev. W.E.P.
Hogg, of St Barnabas' Church, on 'Christianity and Socialism'. ...
These meetings have afforded very great benefit and pleasure to all
who have been able to attend them."

In December 1906 the magazine recorded that "a Bible Class
for Servants is held every Sunday afternoon by Miss Foster at the
Institute. ... Mrs Hobson and Mrs Long hold a Sewing Class for
Girls on Friday evenings, and would be glad to welcome any girls of
fourteen years old and upwards."

Lest it should seem that activities at the Institute were run entirely
by well-meaning middle-class parishioners, it is worth noting that –
continuing the local tradition of self-help – the enterprising women
of Hayfield Road ran a Clothing Club there in the 1920s. And the
children of Hayfield Road were quite capable of organising their own
entertainments. One resident recalled more than 60 years later:

*Edie Dean got all the children to put on a show. We practised
every night under her lamp-post, and when we were ready we
gave a performance at the Institute. The money was given to
a home for blind children. ... Edie was a nice-looking girl. One
night she climbed out of her bedroom window and ran away
from home. She went to London and became a film star. She
came back to visit Hayfield Road a few times. We were all very
impressed by her leopard-skin coat.*

23

From the Daisy Club to Maggie's Club ...

EDIE DEAN'S VARIETY show must have been performed on the stage in the hall at the back of the Institute, which was designed by Mr Fred Openshaw, a local architect, and built in 1928. The total cost of £3,000 was paid by another parishioner, Mrs Rashdall (the childless widow of the Very Revd. Hastings Rashdall, a Fellow of New College and a distinguished moral philosopher). The Vicar anxiously recorded in the parish

magazine: "I have asked Her Highness Princess Marie Louise to come and perform the opening ceremony, and this she has graciously promised to do in November. Between now and then we shall want about 200 chairs, stage curtains and a piano." Donations to the Furnishing Fund ranged from £5 given by Lady Teignmouth to two shillings and sixpence contributed by "Anon".

The hall was duly opened on 21 November 1928 by the Princess. A concert followed the opening ceremony, featuring Miss Orrea Pernel, "a brilliant violinist", and songs sung by the Hon. W. Brownlow. Soon afterwards, according to the parish magazine, the Daisy Club began its new season. This club had 56 members, 34 of whom were in domestic service. It ran a Lending Library and a full programme of dances, suppers, drama classes, and entertainments. Cubs, Brownies, Guides, and Scouts were also based at the Institute. Mrs Joyce Newman recalled in 2004: "I became a Brownie at the age of 7 [in 1931], and we used to meet in the Hall. We often went out on summer evenings and took our tea on to Port Meadow."

By 1939, fifty years after its foundation, the Institute had proved its worth by serving the entire community – not only the working men, or the congregation of St Margaret's Church, but everyone resident in the neighbourhood. But then, in the darkest days of the Second World War, it acquired a new role. In 1940, after the evacuation from Dunkirk, 45,000 soldiers from all over the British Isles were camped on Port Meadow nearby. Mr and Mrs Openshaw and their daughter Peggy, who lived on the corner of Polstead Road and Woodstock Road, conceived the idea of organising social evenings in the hall at St Margaret's Institute to entertain the men. And so "Maggie's Club" was born ...

150,000 cups of tea

FUNDED BY DONATIONS from friends of the Openshaws, club nights were held every Monday, Wednesday, and Friday for the next five years. Entrance was free to members of the armed forces, and local people were also welcomed. Refreshments were served (tea, buns, chocolates, and cigarettes), and there was dancing to the music of Victor Sylvester (at  78 rpm on a radiogram). The club was a huge success. The camp on Port Meadow eventually closed down, but the Royal Army Medical Corps was billeted at St Hugh's College in St Margaret's Road, and "Maggie's" continued in being, serving nurses and orderlies, as well as RAF personnel from nearby aerodromes. The Openshaw family had two main helpers: Miss Hancock, a lady in her seventies who lived at 19 Chalfont Road, and Mrs E. Badham, who lived at 11 Frenchay Road. Violet Ford, who served in the Women's Auxiliary Air Force, is recorded as saying in 1941, "St Margaret's is the friendliest and jolliest place I have been to in Oxford", and Private Johnny Ball asked rhetorically in 1943: "What would Oxford be without Maggie's?"

For some time during the war, the club co-existed with classes of Thomas Road Central School, which had been evacuated from London. Martin Koretz, who attended it from 1942 to 1944, remembers:

In winter there was a large open coal fire in the main hall on the ground floor. The headmaster, Mr Davis, used to take lessons in this hall and always stood with his back to the roaring fire. We

25

Masonic Club Farewell, June 1945

*always noticed the smell of smouldering trousers, while all of us
were shivering with cold. ... At the time there was a tuck shop
on the corner of Aristotle Lane, and the boys would race out at
break time to buy "Fatty Cakes", oozing with fat. They can't have
done me much harm, as I have weighed only a little over 8 stone
for the whole of my adult life.*

By June 1945, Maggie's Club had held 838 sessions, and *The Oxford
Times* printed the following report:

Presentations at farewell dance
St Margaret's Hall, Oxford, was the scene of a farewell dance for
the Forces last night, when "Maggie's", the club which Mr. F.E.
Openshaw, Mrs Openshaw, and Miss Peggy Openshaw have
organised for the Forces, held its 838th session.

The RAMC No. 4 Company dance band gave its services.
Mr Openshaw, in a tribute to the help of friends, said that Miss
Hancock, who dealt with the tea, had missed only five evenings
out of the 838 and had poured out 150,000 cups. Mrs Badham had
cut over 60,000 sandwiches and had only missed ten evenings.

Mr Openshaw made presentations on behalf of his family to
them and to Mrs Badham, Miss Judy Thorne, and Mr Geoffrey
Turner. Miss Mollie Goodall had collected from the Service men
and members of the club, and from these gifts presentations were
made by Colonel Maguire, RAMC, to Miss Peggy Openshaw,
Mr Openshaw, Mrs Openshaw, Miss Hancock, Mrs Badham,
Mr Badham, Mr Geoffrey Turner, and Miss Judy Thorne.

On 21 June 1945, 14 demobilised servicemen who were returning to
their homes all around the British Isles wrote the following letter to
the Openshaws:

On behalf of our little gang in the corner, we wish to express
our grateful and sincere thanks for the happy and most

enjoyable evening we had on the occasion of the fifth anniversary of "Maggie's".

We all feel sorry to hear that "Maggie's" may have to close in the near future, for deep down in our hearts, memories of "Maggie's" will always remain. Most of us will be homeward bound in the near future, and on our return to civilian life if anyone should enquire as to which University we attended during our stay at Oxford, although our answer will be none, we shall be proud to be able to claim the privilege and pleasure of attending "Maggie's".

It is with the greatest pleasure that we thank you, Peggy, Granny, and the many other kind helpers of "Maggie's" staff for the many happy evenings we have had in the past, and we will always associate "Maggie's" with being the one bright spot in Oxford and a home from home.

Our best wishes to everyone, and may God Bless You All.

Peggy Openshaw (who later married and became Peggy Bainbridge, living at 149 Woodstock Road until her death in 2005 at the age of almost 90) recalled much later: "They were very happy times, and we were very sorry when the club closed. We ended solvent, in spite of charging only one penny for a cup of tea."

Jazz and jumble sales

AFTER THE WAR the Institute's local popularity began to decline. Even the billiards saloon lost its appeal. Part of the reason was the advent of television, and part, perhaps, was the refusal of the trustees to allow the sale of alcohol on the premises. But – as one of the few public buildings in Oxford that was equipped with a stage – it was used occasionally for rehearsals and performances by undergraduate drama groups, among them the famous Experimental Theatre Club, which numbered among its members Kenneth Tynan, Michael Flanders, and Sandy Wilson (who wrote a satirical musical which was performed in the Institute in 1947 and is still remembered by a local retired doctor who had a walk-on part in the production).

The Institute was still being used by student drama groups twenty years later. Another local resident remembers rehearsing *The Cherry Orchard* there (with Maria Aitken as Madame Ranevsky) in about 1966, and Harold Pinter's *The Public Eye and the Private Ear*, both of which were put on at The Oxford Playhouse, and the gory Jacobean melodrama *The Revenger's Tragedy*, which was performed in the cloisters of Christ Church.

By the late 1970s the Institute was becoming shabby and neglected. The congregation of St Margaret's Church had dwindled, the church seemed doomed to close, and a small band of stalwarts had great difficulty in keeping the Institute running. A member of the management committee at that time recalls:

> *The whole building was in a horrific state of repair. There was no money, and the lease, with its attendant dilapidations bill, was due to expire in a few years' time. But amazingly the ground floor was well used by a variety of clubs and groups. My favourite was Civil Defence, who practised measures to protect us from nuclear attack by abseiling down from the balcony in the hall, and trundling stretchers around. ... Once we were able to rent the first floor to d'Overbroeck's tutorial college, we were able to build up a small fund for dilapidations and carry out a few much-needed repairs. We engaged a resident caretaker, put in a basic heating system, mended the roof, installed children's toilets, and put up a dividing wall in the front room.*

This was the start of an epic programme of refurbishment, described in more detail in the second half of this chapter. Among the beneficiaries of the battles against dry rot and blocked drains was the Balkan Folk Dance Group, which is the longest-established of all the current users of the Institute. For about 40 years the group has used the hall for its weekly gatherings (attended in the early days by ex-prisoners of war from Balkan countries). Twice a year enthusiasts come from all over Britain to dance to live music, often in full traditional costume.

The Polstead Road Playgroup has been based at the Institute since the 1970s. Thirty years later, the parent-run group is still going strong and plays a central role in the local community. Other long-term users include the Tibetan Buddhist Meditation Group, which has been using the centre for weekly meditation meetings and weekend gatherings for almost 20 years.

Humphrey Carpenter's jazz band, *Vile Bodies,* which played regularly at the Ritz Hotel in London, occasionally rehearsed at the Institute in the 1980s. The multi-talented writer, musician, and broadcaster also founded The Mushy Pea Theatre Company – a drama group for children, including his own two daughters, which met at the Institute on Saturday mornings, improvising stories which they gradually built up into full-scale plays for performance in the hall (but presumably not on the stage, which was demolished some time after 1985 to make space for a larger kitchen). His obituary in *The Times* recorded that Humphrey, having written a jazz musical called *Babes* for the Mushy Peas, spent his royalties from the *Mr Majeika* books on taking the entire cast of more than 50 to London for a run of shows at the Shaw Theatre. "If you have an idea that sounds fun," he remarked, "and you can just about afford it, you really have to do it, don't you? Never know how long you've got." Humphrey died in 2005 at the tragically early age of 58 – a great loss to the local community.

The Institute (when not being used as a polling station at election time) has been, and still is, host to an extraordinary variety of groups, from Alcoholics Anonymous ("The Institute is an invaluable asset to the community", says the Secretary) to the Limes Club day centre, run by the charity Daybreak Oxford, which has used the Institute twice weekly since the mid-1980s, providing day care for older people with mental-health problems or memory loss. ("We provide a friendly club, a supportive environment, a hot lunch, and mentally stimulating activities. We also give some respite for carers.")

Local residents' associations use the hall for public meetings and social events ("It is our second home" – Secretary of the Waterside Residents' Association). Until recently, Suzuki violin classes were held for local children, led by a teacher who lived on a narrowboat on the canal nearby; their twice-yearly concerts raised several hundred pounds for the NSPCC and the Oxfordshire Association for the Blind (shades of Edie Dean!). The Institute has hosted community planning exercises and political hustings. Retired people enjoy Two O'Clock Talks on every subject under the sun. There are classes in Tai Chi, Yoga, Judo, and Pilates ... tango classes ... cello lessons  ... a chess club and a bridge club ... jumble sales ... wine-tastings ... music sessions for pre-school children ... Christmas carols with mince pies and punch ... New Year's Eve parties ...Valentine's Day dances ... There is always something going on. The list seems endless and is ever-changing.

One thing, however, has not changed since the very foundation of the Institute in 1890, and that is the unsung contributions of the many volunteers who keep it running – from the members of the management committee who take the difficult financial decisions to the folk who turn up to wield paintbrushes when the place needs redecorating. It is all done cheerfully, in a spirit of good will, and Violet Ford, if she could come back today, might indeed repeat her words, uttered in 1941: *"St Margaret's Institute is the friendliest and jolliest place I have been to in Oxford".*

PART 2: THE INSTITUTE – ITS RISE, FALL, AND RISE AGAIN

1889: a 99-year lease for the Working Men's Institute

ON 23 JUNE 1891, the President and Scholars of St John's College, Oxford, signed a lease for a piece of land at the end of Polstead Road, next to the Anchor Inn. The St Philip and St James Working Men's Institute, as it was originally called, was the first building to be constructed in Polstead Road: it opened in 1890 – prior to the signing of the lease!

The lease was to run for 99 years from 10 October 1889, and in 1891 that must have seemed a comfortably long stretch. The purpose of the lease was not made explicit in the original indenture, but it was well established that the building was to provide facilities for the local community – in particular for working men.

Trustees continued to be appointed as and when necessary, both from the local churches – SS Philip and James, and St Margaret (completed in 1893) – and from the local community. The system seems to have worked perfectly well until after the Second World War, when the Institute committee, having for so long focused on its tremendous wartime effort (described in the first half of this chapter), perhaps just ran out of steam. Whatever the reason, by 1952 the Trustees had ceased to function. Finally, in 1964, the Diocesan Board of Finance took over as Custodian Trustee, with the Parochial Church Council (PCC) of St Margaret's Church as Administrative Trustee. The future of the Institute was secured – but only in legal terms.

In 1974 there was correspondence with St John's College about the renewal of the lease, which was due to expire in 1988. The College Bursar responded in 1975, but at that stage the PCC seemed to be looking only at an extension of the lease "for another 25 years or something like that", not at an outright purchase.

100 years on: the low point

BY 1984 THE Institute was in a sad state. According to Romy Briant, in a letter to the committee: "The building had a high wooden fence with enclosed concrete yard to which there was no public access ... there was a small kitchen where water dripped on to bare wires. The hall was painted in greys and browns, with large locked cupboards spread around the walls, and there was one urinal, which smelt. The building was in a state of disrepair and there was rampant dry rot ... there were four regular community users in the hall, and a church group or two in the small room."

At this unpromising stage in its history, the Institute had the good fortune to find a champion in Dorothy Metcalf, then church warden, who spoke up for its retention at a time when the PCC could see no future in it. A new committee was set up by the Vicar of St Margaret's, Rev. John Gawne-Cain, and they began to "grapple with the problem" (in the words of David Smith, church warden). They held public meetings, liaised with health and social services, talked with voluntary groups. The consensus was that the Institute should be totally renovated and, by encouraging local users, would once again be a catalyst for the community life of the area. The PCC gave its full support to this new initiative.

There was a burst of confident activity. Public meetings and regular users' meetings were called, and teams of volunteers were involved in epic hall-painting and garden-laying sessions. The Diocese gave some financial support, but most of the money required was raised from other sources. The present lay-out of the rooms on the ground floor, including the creation of the large kitchen in the former "back-stage" area, is the result of that 1987 initiative. The design was the work of students at the new Oxford Brookes University.

There was sadness about losing the stage, which held wartime memories for so many people, but it had been unused for a long time and Humphrey Carpenter (then setting up the Mushy Pea Theatre – a drama group for local children) was clear that he would not use it.

33

1987: the Institute rises from the ashes and negotiates a further 12-year lease

AS 1987 DREW on, it became imperative to negotiate a renewal of the 99-year lease, which was due to end in October 1988. The committee, led by Richard and Romy Briant, were able to reflect with some pride on the enormous improvements in the Institute's facilities and community outreach that their labours had brought about. A 12-year lease was negotiated, but there is a sense in the  archived correspondence that neither side wanted to bring the question of the long-term future of the Institute to a head. The committee continued to make improvements – new lighting, new flooring, and a gallery in the hall – and it encouraged more users to rent space.

By the early to mid-1990s the Institute was again flourishing. In 1996 it was possible for the first time to employ a co-ordinator to take over the day-to-day running of the Institute. In 1999 the new Vicar of St. Margaret's, the Rev. Dr. Andrew Bunch, increased the membership of the committee and, under the chairmanship of Ben Simpson, the Institute moved into a new phase.

2000: the start of negotiations to secure the Institute's future

FOR THOSE CONCERNED for the future of the Institute, the year 2000 marked not only the new millennium but also, on 9 October, the expiry of the Institute's 112-year lease. There appeared to be a very real likelihood that this building, the hub of the community for more than a century, would be repossessed and redeveloped by St. John's. There was clearly no time to waste, and in the spring of 2000 negotiations for the future of the Institute began in earnest.

At the same time, Adele Smith was appointed as the Institute's co-ordinator, her brief being to build up the regular use of the Institute. She encouraged and skillfully managed an astonishing growth in activity over the years that followed, and this enabled the committee to assert confidently that the Institute was a much-needed and well-used resource.

A survey carried out under the terms of the lease meant that the new committee faced a potential bill of more than £20,000 for dilap-idations to the building at the end of the lease.  Negotiations with St John's secured agreement for a year's grace and, under the direction of John Ashby, the committee's honorary building adviser, a programme of contracted and voluntary works commenced, resulting in the first phase of the face-lift that was to follow, and the reparations necessary to satisfy St John's. Between 1999 and 2004 the dilapidations were made good and the structure of the building was made safe. This included repairing the drains and the (very hazard-ous) business of mending the chimneys. In February 2001 the Institute received a £15,000 legacy from local resident Jinner Snodgrass, which made it possible for John Ashby to undertake this work.

The legal situation in 2000 was that St John's could repossess the Institute if it required it for its own occupation, or for redevelopment, or if the management committee had substantially failed to comply with the various covenants in the 1988 lease. Otherwise the Institute was entitled to a new lease, but legally this could be for a maximum of only 14 years – and no more.

On 3 June 2000 a Consultation Day was held at the Institute, which was well attended by local people. A ripple of concern began to spread through the community about the future of local and chari-table activities in the Institute. On 14 June 2000 the committee put to St John's the case for allowing the Institute to survive: the current population of the parish was some 7,000 to 9,000 people, a figure that was likely to grow by some 20–25 per cent in the near future, as a result of the huge building programme on the brown-field land between Oxford railway station and Wolvercote. In a letter of 11 June the committee had said: "We are therefore keen that the whole of the building, which was built, extended and improved by funds contributed voluntarily, should remain available for community purposes. We would if possible like to purchase the freehold."

The outcome of the meeting was the offer by St John's of a five-year extension – which would not be long enough, Ben Simpson argued, to persuade trusts and statutory agencies to fund work at the Institute: "No one will be interested when the planning horizon is as short as five years." Moreover, the five-year lease was to apply to the ground floor alone, with the expectation that any further lease of the ground floor would be at the full commercial value of the property. Fortunately the committee succeeded in negotiating a ten-year lease, with a break clause after five years.

In September 2000 the PCC ratified the committee's negotiation, resolving that the new ten-year lease should be entered into with St John's as a holding position, while the terms of a long lease/purchase proposal were worked out. In early 2004 this resulted in an agreement to purchase a 999-year lease of the Institute from the College, with the object of providing a building for the use of the whole community. The cost of the  purchase was fixed at £400,000, payable in three installments over a four-year period.

During the crucial period from 2000 to 2004, stability was brought to the Institute's finances, and to the Appeal, by two treasurers: firstly Diana Ashby, and secondly (from November 2000 to January 2003) Genefer Clark.

2004: the Appeal is launched

THE COMMITTEE THEN began an Appeal to raise the funds necessary both for the purchase and for essential renovation. Events were organised in and around the Institute, to increase its profile in the community and to raise funds. Some of these have become annual fixtures: Variety Evenings; the Valentine's Ball (now called the Spring Ball); concerts; wine-tastings; Art Week displays; open-gardens days; New Year's Eve parties. Particular mention should be made of the Promises Auctions, to which numerous people have donated promises ranging from dog walking to weeks in holiday cottages.

At a meeting of the city council's North Area Committee in May 2004, Ben Simpson referred to the "one in a thousand year opportunity" to purchase the 999-year lease. Councillor Alan Armitage described the Institute as a "beacon of light" which needed to be recognised and supported (*Oxford Times*, 21 May 2004). The council members were persuaded, and they voted to make a grant to the project.

Since 2004, Bryan Wardley, with the unstinting help of Tony Clear, has managed the modernisation of the building. Much of the hard labour has been provided by local residents, working alongside committee members. A Certificate from the Oxford Preservation Trust was awarded for the excellence of the refurbishments.

2008: the final push

THE APPEAL FOR the lease raised £50,000 from grants and £100,000 from lettings, while £250,000 was raised from local residents, businesses, and fund-raising events. Substantial support and an offer of underwriting came from Oxford City Council. Most importantly, members of the local community were prepared to dig into their pockets, as their predecessors had done in the 1890s. In all, 62.5 per cent of the total £400,000 came from local people, many of whom joined the "400 Club" – the creation of the Institute's Treasurer and indefatigable fundraiser, Bryan Wardley.

The committee decided to revive a historical precedent: the names of the 400 Club have been inscribed on boards in the Institute, as their predecessors' names were in the 1890s.

In April 2008 the final installment of the lease-purchase monies was paid to St John's, and the community breathed a collective sigh of relief: a thousand years is a long time. But the Appeal goes on ... and money is still being raised from local people, as it was 120 years ago, to ensure that the Institute remains at the centre of our community and continues to provide for its changing needs.

6 A School: "Phil & Jim"

NORTH OXFORD, AND in particular St Margaret's Parish, has experienced two waves of development: the first in the 1860s and the second in the 1990s. There was a crucial difference in the way that these developments were each experienced, and this may be because, in the first wave, St John's College exercised a guiding hand on the developers. St John's, and Victorian society in general, appear to have understood that a new suburb needs institutions – a church, a

Artist David Gosling working with Phil & Jim children on the creation of a unicorn for Oxfordshire Art Weeks 2009

39

school, a community hall, for example – if it is to develop a life of its own.

In the second wave of development there appears to have been no such thinking and, as a result, the four housing developments on the west side of the canal were built with no shop, no church, no pub – in fact no central hub around which people could naturally congregate.

St Margaret's Church, helped by both the Diocese and St John's College, responded to this need, and as a result the whole parish, old and new, now has a renewed community centre, better church facilities, and one huge plus: the new Primary School of St Philip and St James: "Phil & Jim", which was relocated from Leckford Road to Navigation Way in 2004. The local children who attend it literally bridge the gap between the old world of St Margaret's and the new world of Waterside when they run across Aristotle Bridge to school.

This chapter outlines the history of Phil & Jim School, which has educated the children of this neighbourhood from its first development in the 1870s to the present time.

* * *

When the site for Phil & Jim School, as it has always been known, was excavated in Leckford Road in 1872, a grave was found: that of a Briton or a Dane, probably buried in a sitting position (because his skull was found lying between his knees). The skeleton was removed, the archaeologists moved on, and the school, intended only for infants, was ready within a year. It opened in 1873, admitting boys and girls between the ages of 3 and 7. In 1879 it was enlarged to cater for boys until the national school-leaving age of 14 (except for the very brightest, who transferred to Oxford High School for Boys at the age of 11). The girls moved at the age of 7 to St Giles' School or the Convent School in St Giles (known as St Denys), which moved to Winchester Road in 1876.

The motive force behind Phil & Jim was E. C. Dermer, vicar of SS Philip and James from 1872 to 1900. He was one of nature's fixers and served as a conduit between his parishioners and the powers of St John's College. The architect was the Gothic Revivalist H. G. W. Drinkwater, who was shortly to design St Margaret's Church, and it is likely that the original school building was constructed in the attractive English vernacular style which he employed in other Oxford buildings. Unfortunately the rebuilding of 1896, and additions in 1933 and 1966, resulted in a collection of interlinked red-brick sheds which could have done nothing for the children's sense of their value to the community.

But what Phil & Jim *would* have given these children was a sense of stability in a suburb which was continually transforming itself – both for the tradespeople on the Kingston Road side and for the gentry on the Woodstock Road side. The school kept the round of church festivals, with holidays on saints' days and an afternoon off for St Giles' Fair (a custom which should perhaps be revived?), and so the children would have experienced the continuity of a more settled society in a world that was to change utterly in the years between 1872 and 1918, and 1945, and 2010.

In October 1874 the school inspector reported that "the school is taught with great kindness and in many respects with skill". So, although there were less positive comments about the children's handwriting and arithmetic, it would appear that the school succeeded in its essential purpose. Even in the 1880s it appears to have been innovative. For instance, there were "Object Lessons" given in the galleries (tiers of desks at each end of the big schoolroom), when talks with demonstrations were given on an eclectic range of topics: for example, "A camel", "The colour yellow", "Sugar", and "The cube".

Every child went home for dinner during a two-hour break, and often if the weather was bad they would not return in the afternoon. The children wore clothes that were difficult to dry, and there was real concern about minor illnesses becoming serious. On occasions when the pupils got very wet, the teachers would spend the rest of the day building up fires in the stoves to dry out their clothes. There were outbreaks of measles, scarlet fever, and diphtheria, and infant mortality was a reality. In February 1889, the log-book records: "Three children died who were all present at school last Friday".

A reason for both the stability of the school and its steady improvement in the first half of the twentieth century was its well-loved and respected headmaster George Dent, known as "Gaffer Dent", who led the school from 1902 to 1946. The story goes that the vicar took Mr Dent, dressed in his smartest suit and "hard billycock hat", to the school gate, gestured at the throng inside and said, "Do what you like. Make a good clearance. And don't see me for a week." Mr Dent marched in, to be greeted by an astonished silence as the boys gazed at his extraordinary style of dress.

He has been described as "a 'big' man in every sense of the word – a man of power, physically and intellectually". The reports of the school inspectors and his own painstakingly kept log-books record how he raised standards dramatically and improved the school's reputation. His own subject was mathematics, for which he found practical applications: measuring the playground, working out the construction of buildings, and running a tuck shop: skills that would be useful to the boys when they started in the family business, or at the Oxford University Press, or at one of the stores that were establishing themselves in the expanding city centre. Gardening classes were held on the Trap Ground allotments, and wood and metal work classes were given for 45 years by Mr Cox – described as a "mechanical genius", always "putting models together in class" or "building those steam engines that run on methylated spirit".

There was a custom, which lasted at least 25 years, for a boy to run out of school at break to buy slabs of lardy cake at one penny a slice from Blencowe's bakery in Kingston Road. He then had to sneak back into the playground, for of course if he was caught he would be caned. It seems to have been a risk worth taking.

Mr Dent had planned to retire in 1939, but the outbreak of war put paid to that. Although the school appears to have been very little affected by the First World War, apart from the employment of more women staff, the Second World War was to present a bigger challenge. There was an immediate influx of 27 children from the Cowley Poor Law School, evicted to make room for evacuees; and four days later Mr Dent found that he also had to accommodate a school of London evacuees, aged 11 to 16 and "bigger, tougher, and poorer" than his own pupils. The two schools worked half a day each, and the evacuees were billeted in houses and a hostel in the streets around the school; the task of hosting them was described by Mr Davis, a later head teacher, as an "extremely challenging and voluntary selfless duty".

In the fifty years after the Second World War there were many changes in the life of Phil & Jim. The great challenge appears to have been the need to provide a full range of education for children from infancy to school-leaving age. In North Oxford there was no secondary school, and so children who failed to obtain places in selective schools stayed at Phil & Jim and the other "primary" schools until they reached the school-leaving age, which was raised to 15, but with no additional resources made available.

Attempts were made to provide specialist subject teaching for the older boys, but these seem to have been foiled by the large class sizes, and by the pupils' differing abilities. Science equipment was limited to a demonstration bench with simple apparatus and one or two bunsen burners, but the boys did do some work on the making of coal gas, which was followed by a visit to the Gas Works. Valiant efforts were made to introduce them to the world of work: there were trips to the blood-transfusion centre at the Churchill Hospital, Lucy's Eagle Ironworks, Cooper's Marmalade Factory, Job's Dairy, and the *Oxford Mail* Printing Works. The younger children do seem to have been well catered for, with a great variety of activities: music classes, dance displays, gym, art, and craftwork.

It was not until 1963 that the Cherwell Secondary Modern School opened, taking the 11-plus boys from Phil & Jim. At that point the primary-school girls from St Denys moved to Phil & Jim, which became wholly co-educational for the first time in its history. In 1965, when the Oxfordshire school system adopted the three-tier model, there was a further sea-change as Phil & Jim was transformed into a first school for 5–9 year olds,

Teaching styles changed as time moved on, but the good reputation of the school was always maintained. However, the restricted site was becoming an increasing problem: what had seemed fine for 241 infants and boys in 1911 was not considered adequate for 200 children three generations later.

At this stage, there was a possibility of moving the school out of North Oxford to the site of the former Bishop Kirk Middle School in Summertown. This proposal was not universally welcomed, and when the Aristotle Lane industrial estate came up for re-development a new site for the school was sought in that area. A land swap was arranged: the Bishop Kirk site for the Aristotle Lane site. At this stage the three-tier system was ending, and Phil & Jim became a full primary school again in September 2003.

The foundation stone for the new school was laid on 11 April 2002 by Bishop Richard Harries. The hall has a magnificent aquamarine Noah's Ark window, made by local stained-glass artist Susan Moxley, which was a gift from St Margaret's Church to the new school.

The transition to the new buildings came just as Phil & Jim started to grow into its new primary-school status, so the first children to move in were the ten-year-old cohort, but by early 2004 the whole school had come together on the new site. Fortunately this transition period has been overseen by one head of school, Irene Conway, whose leadership at this critical time has been assisted by a very able team of staff and governors. The result is that the school has consistently grown not only in numbers (the maximum now is 420) but also in the standard of education on a broad front. In 2010 the school's performance and capacity for the arts was judged outstanding for Artsmark. The school was recently rated in an Ofsted report as "good, with outstanding features". At the time of writing, the children speak 21 first languages between them, and the school's SATS (Standard Assessment Tests) and "value added" scores are at the top of the Oxfordshire league tables.

The children are involved in all sorts of activities – for instance the creation of willow sculptures for a glade in the Trap Grounds (including a life-size unicorn whose theft from an Oxford Castle display in May 2010 caused great dismay). In March 2010 the winner of an anti-cyber-bullying cartoon competition was a pupil at Phil & Jim, and in July 2010 the pupils won an Osca award from the County for a project in which the children monitored energy use in the classroom.

The children who now attend the school are drawn both from the traditional catchment area and also from the new estates developed around the new school buildings. The school is, rightly, very popular. But, as a result, there is a new educational issue to be confronted: how can enough places be found for all the children of the community? No doubt Phil & Jim will find a solution.

7 A Street: Hayfield Road

BEFORE HAYFIELD ROAD as we know it was developed in 1886–1888, it was a muddy lane, known at least until the early 18th century as "The Upper Way to Wolvercote", and from the middle of that century as "Heyfields Hut Lane" (or variants on that name, such as "The Hut", and even "The Hat", on early Ordnance Survey maps). There were some old cottages on the west side of the lane, with gardens extending to the canal. The Census for 1841 records 12 families living in "Heyfields Hutt" (apart from the family of Anthony Harris, the

Heyfields Hut Lane, sketched in pencil, c. 1832

inn-keeper at The Anchor). The breadwinners consisted of four agricultural labourers, a millwright, a carpenter, a clay-pipe maker, and five boat builders, who presumably worked at the boatyard half-way along the lane which appears in a map dated 1846, commissioned by the London, Oxford, and Cheltenham Railway.

An article in the *Clarendonian* magazine of 1923, recalling Walton Manor in the 1860s, described the cottages as "very old and dilapidated". Henry Minn, recalling his childhood in the 1870s, described the cottages as squalid and stated that the inhabitants made a living from selling firewood. The records of St Giles's Parish reveal a high rate of infant mortality among the shifting population of the lane.

Conditions improved greatly in the late 1880s, when the Oxford Industrial and Provident Land and Building Society laid out the modern roadway and built a street of "model artisans' cottages ... sound and healthy dwellings, to let at moderate rents".

The suburb that never was

WHY DOES HAYFIELD Road, with its uniform terraces of plain brick houses, look so incongruous among the Victorian Gothic villas of North Oxford? The answer is that it was originally intended to be part of a grid of identical streets, housing the families of several hundred employees of the wagon works that the Great Western Railway proposed to establish on Cripley Meadow.

In October 1865, *Jackson's Oxford Journal* reported that St John's College, owner of most of the land hereabouts, had instructed its architects to draw up plans for "the requisite residences on college land beyond Heyfield's Hutt". The editor confidently predicted that "a new suburb will shortly be springing up". But the developers and the *Journal* had reckoned without the powerful conservative lobby in Oxford. The University, dismayed at the prospect of Oxford becoming a manufacturing town, brought pressure to bear in the right quarters, and the wagon works were eventually built in Swindon instead.

Plans for the new suburb were shelved for 20 years, and when eventually they were taken off the shelf and dusted down, only one road was built – mainly to house the families of labourers who were moving in from outlying villages to work on the construction of grand villas for academic and professional people. The community of North Oxford was expanding rapidly at the time. So in 1885 St John's leased land in Heyfield Road to the Oxford Industrial and Provident Land and Building Society for the construction of houses, designed by H. Wilkinson Moore, the college's architect, for lease to the Society's members at prices ranging from £170 to £176. At the same time, the Canal Company was improving the wharf, and St John's was transforming The Hut public house, of dubious repute, into what the *Journal* described as "a picturesque wayside inn".

In October 1888 the *Journal* reported that the Oxford Industrial and Provident ("that flourishing and useful society") had completed the building of "a whole street of model artisans' dwellings". Most of the leases were taken on by tradespeople who lived elsewhere and sub-let the houses to poorer families. The Blencowe sisters, for instance, the four daughters of the baker in Kingston Road, acquired one house each in Hayfield Road, for sub-letting.

Ann and Agabus Green: links with the past

AGABUS GREEN, A builder's labourer born in Botley, lived with his wife Ann, a laundress, and their five children in one of the old dilapidated cottages in Hayfield Hutt Lane in the 1870s. They moved to live in the relative comfort of a new house in the street when it was re-built in 1886–88. Mr Green was one of the first elected sidesmen at St Margaret's Church, "to which he was loyally devoted", according to the parish magazine after he died in 1901: he was one of the oldest residents of the community, who "possessed the respect and regard of all who came into contact with him".

The new community

THE CENSUS FOR 1891, the first taken after the building of the new Hayfield Road was complete, recorded the occupations of the residents. Most of the men worked on building sites and coal yards as labourers, or at the University Press in Walton Street as type founders, or on the railways as porters or signalmen. The young lads were mostly employed as errand boys or servants. Young unmarried women worked as domestic servants or dressmakers, and some older women as sick nurses or laundresses. Most wives were fully occupied in raising their families. The biggest family was the Chappells at number 80, with ten children ranging in age from 7 months to 12 years (the five eldest girls rejoicing in the names Rose, Lillie, Daisy, Violet, and Myrtle).

Life was hard in the days when manual workers were not paid when laid off in bad weather. A Relief Committee established by St Margaret's Church appealed in 1911 for "gifts of men's clothes suitable for emigrants to Australia", and "a purchaser for the following items, to help their owner raise funds towards emigration: a treadle sewing machine, a banjo, and a child's mail-cart". One family who took their chances in Australia were the Pitmans from number 22.

Ada Tombs

ADA TOMBS WAS born at 3 Hayfield Road in 1890 and was still living there when she died in 1971. She worked in a college kitchen and kept house for her brothers, William and Thomas. Local people recall her prim and proper ways ("she scrubbed her front door-step every day of her life"). Passing canal boatmen used to throw their boots into her garden for Tommy the "shoe-snob" to mend, and they would collect them on their return journey.

49

The life and times of the Goddard family

A VIVID ACCOUNT of life in Hayfield Road before the First World War
was given to the author in 1993 by Miss Florrie Goddard, a relation
of the Goddard family who had moved into number 53 when it was
first built. Edwin Goddard (born 1856) was a police constable, and
his wife Esther worked as a cleaner in nearby big houses. She would
take the smallest of her eight children with her and, when they were
old enough, the boys used to go round the houses in Chalfont Road
before school to lay fires and clean shoes. They each earned one
shilling a week from their "morning places", and they had to put the
money in a savings bank. The children went to Phil & Jim School in
Leckford Road, and the family attended St Margaret's Church.

Edwin Goddard, born at the Nut Tree Inn at Murcott on Otmoor,
never forgot his country origins. He had a half-share in a cow on Port
Meadow, some rough shooting on Boar's Hill, and several allotments
in Marston Ferry Road. There was often rabbit pie for dinner, and
one of the children would be sent down town to Warburton's in The
Friars to sell the skin for twopence. Another boy would be sent to
Butler's in Park End Street with a sack to fill up with bread, as it
was a ha'penny cheaper there. Mr Goddard kept ducks, hens, rabbits,
ferrets, and bees in the back garden of number 53. With milk from
the cow Mrs Goddard would make butter by shaking the cream in a
big glass sweet bottle.

The boys were each given a shilling as soon as they could swim both
ways across the canal at the bottom of the garden. Florrie described
calling at the house one day with her mother. They pushed open the
front door and went in. Suddenly all the boys came running in from
the canal stark naked, to the horror of Florrie's mother.

One unforgettable night PC Goddard, returning home up Walton
Street in the early hours of the morning, discovered a fire at the
University Press. He gave the alarm, and little damage was done.
Next day the Printer sent for him to offer him a reward. PC Goddard
said he had four sons at home and would be grateful if jobs could be

found for them. So William and Edwin and Herbert and Stan started work at the Press, where they stayed all their working lives, like several other residents of Hayfield Road.

Between the wars

"HAYFIELD ROAD WAS like one big family in the old days. Nobody ever locked their front doors." ..."You couldn't lead a double life in the Hayfield Road. We all knew one another's business." The memories of the oldest residents (recorded by the author in 1993) are testament to the strong sense of community in the street. On summer evenings, while the men were playing dominoes at The Anchor, the women would put chairs out on the pavement and sit gossiping outside their front doors as the children played in the dusk. "We used to throw up our hats to catch bats", one man recalled. "What we used to sing was: 'Bat! Bat! Come into my hat!'"

Childhood was short in the years between the wars – the school-leaving age was 14 – and money was short, too. But the children of Hayfield Road knew how to entertain themselves. "In the school holidays, we played on Port Meadow from dawn to dusk ... We fished for newts with a worm on the end of a string ... We used to put ha'pennies on the railway line, so the trains would flatten them and make them look like pennies ... We had bonfires and roasted potatoes ... We used to roam across the river to Binsey, with jam sandwiches and bottles of water, the older ones looking after the little ones ... When the fish train came by from Grimsby at 8 pm, that was the signal to go home."

The children had their own cricket team, captained by Molly Harris ("the best cricketer of them all", everyone agreed). They played on the Aristotle Lane "Rec" against teams from Jericho. "We could never afford new equipment. But Mr Kidd, the bank manager from Chalfont Road, used to pay us to give him batting practice. If we bowled him out, he gave us sixpence, or an old leather ball."

Charlie Giles and Little Mush

CHARLIE GILES, OF 72 Hayfield Road, was a deputy station master for the Great Western Railway. He always wore a flower in his button-hole, and always tipped his hat to the war memorial by St Margaret's Church as he cycled home from work ("even when he was drunk"). He was friendly with Haile Selassie, the Emperor of Abyssinia, who, when living in England in exile from 1936 to 1941, used to wait in Charlie's office for the London train. Charlie was once reported for swearing at the Duke of Marlborough ("but the Duke swore at him first").

ARTHUR LEWIS ("LITTLE Mush") was a solitary man who lived in a shed named Tingewick in Frog Lane in the 1930s. Gassed on active service in World War I, he lived alone, isolated from the world by a severe speech impediment. He had a shotgun, three cats, and a spiteful goose ("to ward off The Social", according to local people who remembered him). He used to pick coals from the railway line, and was always filthy. ("Once his sister persuaded him to go and live with her in Reading, but she made him have a bath, so he came back the next day.") He continued to live in the hut, and Charlie Giles' family took him Christmas dinner every year until he died.

"Life was never dull in Hayfield Road"

THERE WAS ALWAYS something happening in the street. On Wednesdays cows were driven down the road from Wolvercote to Gloucester Green market. On Saturdays an Italian hurdy-gurdy man came round, with a monkey that held out a tin for coins. Once a year everyone enjoyed donkey rides and coconut shies at the Radiators Fête (in the grounds of the factory where the Waterways estate now stands). There were grand fancy-dress parties in the street to celebrate the silver jubilee of George V and the coronation of George VI.

There was great excitement in September each year, when the show-men from St Giles's Fair camped with their families and horses and caravans in what is now Bainton Road. The children of Hayfield Road, forbidden by their parents to stray too close, were irresistibly drawn to the caravans – but they were disappointed in one respect: "We saw the acrobats and the dancing girls with their hair in curlers. They didn't look a bit glamorous!"

On one memorable night, there was a fire at Wooldridge & Simpson's wood-yard near the canal in Frenchay Road. "The sky was all lit up, and you could feel the heat all the way down the street. Mr Soden [the chimney sweep from 73 Hayfield Road] ran up and down the street ringing a bell. The wood was lost, but all the horses were saved." And there was the never-forgotten day when Charlie Giles' pig fell in the canal, and just about everyone in the street helped to haul it out.

Canal rescue

"A POLICEMAN DISCOVERED a dog trapped in the icy canal after another dog directed him to the scene. The dog barked at the officer to get his attention and then urged him to follow him to the canal at Hayfield Road, where the second dog was found. The officer managed to pull the struggling dog out of the frozen water, and both dogs barked their thanks and ran off." (*The Oxford Times*, 25 January 1929)

"Somehow Mother always coped"

IF CHILDREN IN Hayfield Road in the 1920s had more freedom than children do today, it is also true that they had more responsibilities. Times were hard, and the young ones were expected to contribute to the household economy. Some earned a few pennies after school by helping to feed and water the canal boatmen's horses in the stables on the wharf; or by fetching beer for the neighbours from the jug-and-bottle hatch at The Anchor.

"My mother used to shell peas for the colleges. We little ones helped her. She used to get three shillings for shelling 100 pounds", one man recalled. "She used to send me to buy the bacon bits left in the slicing machine at Sainsbury's on Saturday nights, and broken biscuits and stale buns (three pence for a carrier-bag full) from Weeks' Bakery in Paradise Square."

Many families kept pigs in their back gardens (in defiance of restrictions imposed by St John's College, the owner of the freeholds). "There was always a side of bacon hanging in our living room", remembered one lady. The children helped to wash the chitterlings and make the brawn. On wash-days they went down to Navigation House with basins to fetch faggots and peas, cooked on her kitchen range by Mary Harris (wife of Albert, the foreman on the wharf).

In some houses in Hayfield Road, every day (except Sunday) was wash-day. Taking in washing for colleges was one of the few ways in which women could earn money. Mrs Phipps, a Keble College scout who lived at number 26, used to bring stiff-fronted shirts by the dozen for her neighbours to wash. At number 90, old Mrs Offoway (born a Kimber in Headington Quarry) would toil all week: soaking, scrubbing, mangling, pegging out, ironing, and goffering. But on Sundays she would take off her apron, don a long black cape and an ostrich-feathered hat, and walk all the way to Forest Hill and back to visit her family.

These women were resourceful all right. Somehow they kept their families clean (the men took baths at the Institute in Polstead Road, but women and children had to go to the public wash-house in Paradise Street, or use a tin bath in front of the fire at home). They ran a clothing club at the Institute. Although most families paid four pence a week to be on the panel of Dr Woods in Dispensary Road (near Gloucester Green), the women acted as midwives to each other, and some of them, when called upon, would lay out the dead. "If you were ever in trouble," everyone remembers, "there was always someone you could call on for help."

And now ...

YOU COULD HAVE bought a house in Hayfield Road for £100 after the First World War. You would have been part of a community in which everyone knew everyone else (and quite likely were related to their neighbours, directly or indirectly). These days, £500,000 will hardly buy you a house in the street. We seem to be preoccupied with our kitchen extensions and loft conversions, and we mostly stay behind our own front doors. Residents who were born in nearby villages such as Yarnton and Wytham have been replaced by newcomers from all over the world. But people still collect their neighbours' children from school, newcomers go shopping for the old people, and gifts of rhubarb from the allotments are still left on front doorsteps (even if the steps are not scrubbed and whitened as faithfully as they once were). May we never lose the neighbourliness for which Hayfield Road was always renowned.

8 A Garage and a Shop: Aladdin and Bunter's

Aladdin: new cars for old

NEXT TO THE Anchor Inn, the Aladdin Garage stands on the site of "very commodious livery stables", so described in an advertisement addressed to gentlemen by John Bridges of Hayfield's Hutt in connection with the Sheriff's Races in 1788. The races were held annually

Aladdin Garage, Hayfield Road, 2010. On the left: Kelvin Chambers

on Port Meadow from at least 1630 for more than 200 years. Ladies and gentlemen, horse dealers and pickpockets, scholars and Punch-and-Judy men flocked there. Assemblies and balls were held in the town during Race Weeks in the eighteenth century, and hairdressers came from London to prepare the ladies' elaborate coiffures. On the Meadow, besides horse racing, there were wrestling and sack races, hog-chasing, and "smock-races" for women in petticoats. Diarist Thomas Hearne complained in 1732 that "Booths and vicious living were there for about seven weeks ...'tis abominable that Poppet shews and Rope dancing should have been this summer in Oxford for more than two months, to the debauching and corrupting of youth."

On the subject of debauchery and the corrupting of youth, in January 1887 Elias Nelms, who ran a hansom-cab business on the Aladdin site, was sued for breach of promise of marriage by Miss Sarah Rayner, a housemaid at Tew Park. But Hayfield Road is *very* respectable these days, and no such accusations can be made against Kelvin Chambers, the managing director, who has run the garage with Gill, his wife, Gareth, his son, Matthew George, the director, and Matthew's wife Bene since 1995. (For 30 years before that, Kelvin had worked part-time for the previous owner, Tom Robinson, who took over from his father-in-law, Bill Abraham, and bought the site from Hall's Brewery. Before that, Harry Denton ran the garage in the 1930s, and used to charge local people sixpence to recharge accumulators from their wireless sets.) Kelvin and his team, ever-cheerful, provide a much-valued local service. If they are occasionally disturbed by the ghost of Harry, a carpenter who once occupied a corner of the site and reputedly hanged himself there, they never show it.

Bunter's Delicatessen

THE SHOP IN Hayfield Road on which the neighbourhood relies for newspapers, milk, and local gossip was originally in 1890 two separate shops: a butcher's and a grocer's. By 1904 both premises were being run as a general store and telegraph office by Mrs

57

Hayfield Road shop, c. 1910

Restall, wife of the wharfinger and haulier whose business was based on the canal wharf opposite. She was succeeded in 1907 by Richard Hall, who sold furniture in number 4 and household goods in number 6 for 20 years. (His name and business are still proclaimed in large fading letters on the south wall of number 4.) For the next 25 years Mr and Mrs Berry traded as confectioners at number 4, while next door was a post office. In 1952 both shops were taken over by the Oxford and Swindon Co-Op, which traded there until 1965, when Mr Snowden ("Snowy") opened his animal and garden supplies shop. When he retired in 1981, his young assist-ant, Lawrence Todd, took over the business, until soaring rents forced him to give up in 1985, whereupon the shop became a delicatessen.

Nicholas Vernicos and his family took over in 1988, intro-ducing Greek food and wine into the local diet. Nicholas presided at the counter with the air of the sea captain he had once been. When he died in 2003, loved and respected by all, his equally popular son Manos inherited the business, working hard with his wife and

Hayfield Road shop, 2010

mother to maintain the deli's reputation for wholesome home-made food, served with a smile.

Since 2009, when Manos sold the business to concentrate on running his shop and café in Walton Street, the shop has been run by Gursharan Saini, known to all as Pete, and his wife Balwinder (Bal). They have increased the range of produce to include traditional Indian dishes, organic and free-trade produce, and (for their customers' everyday needs) everything from lentils to light bulbs. But some commodities have not changed since 1890: local gossip and opinions about the weather.

From coal yard to graphic-design studio

OPPOSITE BUNTER'S AND Aladdin, on the site of the old coal wharf, is Oxford Designers & Illustrators, operating in offices previously occupied by Midland Builders and subsequently by the Open University. Oxford Illustrators and its sister company, Oxford Illustrated Press, moved into 1 Hayfield Road (adopting Aristotle House, Aristotle Lane, as their address) in 1977. (Oxford Illustrators had begun life in 1968 as a small team of technical illustrators working for academic journal publishers; Oxford Illustrated Press published books on transport and of local interest, and was later sold.)

Following the move to the canal bank, a further sister company, Oxprint, was formed. It grew to serve the design, typesetting, and page make-up needs of educational publishers. These companies were financially supported by Blackwell's, who owned the building. At the insistence of the City Council, they were obliged to build four new flats on part of the old wharf. Blackwell's soon sold their part-ownership of the companies to the then Managing Director, and the ownership of the premises passed to Wadham College.

In 1998, members of the current staff took over the ownership of the business, and the new company became Oxford Designers & Illustrators. Peter Lawrence, the current Managing Director, says:

"We may not use the canal for transporting our artwork, but the wharf site has always been a very pleasant place to work."

A cobbler and an ice-cream parlour

SOME OTHER TRADES once carried on in Hayfield Road have long since disappeared. According to Kelly's Trade Directory for 1928, Mrs Elizabeth Bassett ran a sweet shop at number 41; Mr and Mrs Henry Johnson presided over an ice-cream parlour at number 49; and Herbert Pacey ran a dairy shop at number 57. Children would take jugs to be filled up at the dairy for their mothers, and sometimes with the small change they would be allowed to buy home-made ice cream, sprinkled with raspberry vinegar, in two-penny cornets, which they consumed in the Johnsons' front parlour. Mr Soden, the chimney sweep, traded from his home at number 73, opposite a shoe mender at number 88, and not far from a boot maker at number 59.

9 A Town Green: The Trap Grounds

THE TRAP GROUNDS – between the canal and the railway, immediately to the south of the Frenchay Road canal bridge – consists of three acres of reed bed and four acres of scrubland, woodland, and meadow, forming a rich mosaic of wildlife habitats.

The site was owned by St John's College and used as a rubbish tip for nearly 200 years until it was acquired by Oxford City Council in 1965. The name (in recorded use since at least 1832) may derive

Trap Grounds rubbish clearance, 2008

from the practice of trapping birds here ... or the making of eel traps from willow withies ... or the parking of pony-drawn traps during the annual Sheriff's Races on Port Meadow ... or the dumping of night-soil from the "traps" or privies of university colleges. Or it may be a corruption of the designation "Extra Parochial", which denoted the site's exemption (as it lay outside the parish of St Giles) from the payment of church tithes.

Slow-Worms and Glow-Worms

AT LEAST 35 species of bird breed on the Trap Grounds, including seven types of warbler. The reed bed, supporting one of the largest colonies of Reed Warbler to be found within the city boundary, is one of the few places in urban Oxford where cuckoos breed. One particular cuckoo returned to this site for eight successive years, laying a world record of 25 eggs here in 1988. The rarest resident bird is the Water Rail, an elusive creature less often seen than heard: lurking in the reeds, it occasionally gives vent to a series of grunts, yelps, and

squeals, known as "sharming". It is not known to breed anywhere else within the city boundaries.

In grassy places on the scrubland lives Oxford's only known breeding colony of Viviparous Lizards, which may be seen sunning themselves on piles of stones in warm weather. They share the site with Slow-Worms and Glow-Worms. Grass Snakes live in the damp vegetation, sometimes emerging to sunbathe on the

A Water Rail

banks of the stream. The most elusive resident is probably *Nesticus cellulanus,* a rare spider recorded only once elsewhere in Oxford (in the cellar of the Mitre Hotel in the 1920s).

Neglected for many years, by the mid-1990s the reed bed had been invaded by scrub willows and was in danger of drying out, and the scrubland was being used as an unofficial rubbish dump. Despite its somewhat unsavoury aspects, the site was greatly valued by local dog-walkers and bird-watchers. In 1996 a newly constituted group called the Friends of the Trap Grounds mobilised about 50 local volunteers to begin clearing invasive willows from the reed bed, bringing light and air to the reeds, and raising the groundwater level. In 1998 volunteers created a path along the bank of the stream, linking it with an existing path to make a twenty-minute circular walk through several different types of habitat. Tons of rubbish, including a dead caravan, were removed from a filthy swamp, and snowdrops, primroses, and bluebells were planted along the stream. Maintenance work has continued regularly ever since then: the task of keeping paths clear of brambles and the glades clear of rubbish never ceases.

In 2000, grants from the Oxford Preservation Trust and Unipart Ltd. paid for the creation of a pond. The Friends planted hazels, willows, alders, and buckthorns on the banks. Swans have nested and produced cygnets on the pond most years since 2001. Bats skim over it in the dusk. Water Voles lurk among the reeds and are occasionally seen swimming across the open water.

The Town Green campaign

DESPITE ALL THIS, plans were announced for the construction of a road and 45 houses on the scrubland, to add to the total of almost 2000 new houses and apartments which have been built along a two-mile stretch of the "canal corridor" since 1997. Determined to save the site for wildlife and local people, the Friends of the Trap Grounds successfully argued at a public inquiry in 2002 that the scrubland is a Town Green under the terms of the Commons Registration Act (1965), which affirms the right of a local community to the continued use of unfenced land for informal recreation, once the land has been thus used as of right for at least 20 years. But that was not the end of the matter: the case went all the way to the House of Lords, via the High Court and the Court of Appeal. In 2006, the law lords ruled in favour of the Friends. It was a historic verdict, in that it clarified the law and has opened the way for other groups around the country to claim similar open spaces for community use.

Oxfordshire County Council accordingly registered the scrubland as a Town Green and the City Council voted to work together with local people to manage the Trap Grounds for wildlife and recreation. In June 2007 the campaign to save the Trap Grounds from development was recognised with an award presented by the Campaign to Protect Rural England (CPRE).

Now what?

THE WHOLE SITE, now safe from development, is managed by the Friends, in partnership with the City Council, "to conserve and enhance the Trap Grounds as a resource for wildlife, recreation, and education" (to quote the FoTG constitution).

In terms of conservation, over-dominant sycamore trees are being removed, to bring more light into the woodland, and the grassland is being cleared of brambles and invasive alien species to create a wildflower meadow. Bat boxes (made by an 87-year-old partially sighted man, and paid for by the local branch of the Women's Institute) have been installed, and reptile refuges created. To encourage recreation, access is being improved by creating new paths and sunny glades. In 2010 a boardwalk for wheelchair users and families with pushchairs

64

was constructed alongside the stream, to end in a viewing platform overlooking a small reed bed.

In terms of education, at one end of the scale academic zoologists and ornithologists continue to monitor the wildlife of the site, updating records that date back to the 1930s. At the other end of the scale, in 2009 the Friends obtained a Lottery grant to pay an environmental artist to work with children from Phil & Jim School to create giant creatures out of willow: a unicorn, an owl, a dragonfly, and a mysterious egg. The artist himself created a huge version of the Emperor Moth, which breeds on the site. The glade where some of the willow creatures are still displayed has become a space used by classes from Phil & Jim for story telling and creative writing. For members of the general public, the Friends organise occasional bird-song walks, glow-worm expeditions, and moth-trapping nights.

The Friends' website (www.trap-grounds.org.uk), created and managed by local sixth-former Anthony Grieveson, contains news of forthcoming events, the history of the site, the judicial judgements in the Town Green case, lists of all the species present on the site, and a page where visitors can record interesting sightings of wildlife. The reed bed has been officially designated as a County Wildlife Site, and it is hoped that the designation will be extended to cover the scrubland also.

For the future, the Trap Grounds has potential to host a 'Green Gym' scheme. Several such schemes are already running successfully in the county, but so far none in the city. Instead of prescribing medication, local GPs prescribe conservation work in the open air in suitable cases to patients who are suffering from depression or who need physical exercise. The Trap Grounds is an ideal place for such a project, as a suburban site easily accessible by public transport. Whether or not such an official scheme ever comes to fruition, the Trap Grounds will always offer fresh air, peace and quiet, and wild beauty to anyone whose spirits need uplifting.

10 A Famous Son: Lawrence of Arabia

"The first modern celebrity"

All men dream: but not equally. Those who dream by night in the dusty recesses of their minds wake in the day to find it was vanity: but the dreamers of the day are dangerous men, for they may act their dreams with open eyes, to make it possible. This I did.

THOMAS EDWARD LAWRENCE, "The Uncrowned King of Arabia", was eight years old when his family moved in 1896 to 2 Polstead Road, a new house in a new suburb. It was an unconventional household by Victorian standards: his father, Thomas Chapman, was an Anglo-Irish baronet, and his mother, Sarah Lawrence, had been governess to Chapman's four daughters. They eloped, never married, but had five sons, of whom T. E. was the second. Between 1885 and 1896 they moved around – between Dublin, Wales, Scotland, Brittany, Jersey, and the New Forest – presumably always concerned that their unmarried status would be exposed.

Polstead Road, as a new community (the houses were built between 1888 and 1896), would have suited them well. Their secret appears never to have been discovered, probably because they kept themselves to themselves.

Lawrence attended Oxford High School for Boys in George Street between 1896 and 1905. He is remembered locally for having, as a schoolboy, tried to excavate the Round Hill, a Bronze Age burial mound in Port Meadow. In 1906 he made a collection of artefacts from the 16th and 17th centuries from building sites in the city and presented them to the Ashmolean Museum; and in 1908 he master-minded a crazy expedition by canoe through the Oxford sewers to chart the course of the Trill Mill Stream.

Between 1907 and 1910 Lawrence was an undergraduate at Jesus College, although he continued to live at home. In 1908 he persuaded his parents to build a two-room cottage for him in the garden of 2 Polstead Road. The cottage is still there. In the summer of 1909 he journeyed on foot for hundreds of miles across Syria, and the Hittite seals that he collected on this journey can be seen in the Ashmolean, together with his gold-threaded Arab robes.

After completing his degree in 1910, Lawrence worked as an archae-ologist in the Middle East. At the outbreak of war in 1914, he was co-opted by the British Army to serve as an "archeological smoke-screen" for a military survey of the Negev Desert. He was then posted to the Army intelligence staff in Cairo and given a liaison role, devel-oping contacts with the local population. Lawrence swiftly became a trusted adviser to Emir Faisal, the leader of the Arab Revolt against the Turks, who were allies of Germany. He fought with Arab irregu-lars under the command of Faisal in extended guerrilla operations, and in 1918 was involved in the liberation of Damascus. But, after Britain and France carved up the Middle East between them in 1921, he returned home.

Newly elected to a fellowship at All Souls College, Lawrence began to write *The Seven Pillars of Wisdom*. At the same time he was being lionised by an American journalist, Lowell Thomas, who gave public lectures in Britain and the United States about the Arab Revolt, illus-trated by film of Lawrence and Arab tribesmen. Despite his resolute endeavours to bury himself in his writing, and his enlistment at the lowliest level in the Army and then the RAF, Lawrence found himself accorded the status of an international celebrity.

He died in 1935, following a motorcycle accident. Even that had its dramatic effect: the neurosurgeon who attended Lawrence, Hugh Cairns (later appointed first Nuffield Professor of Surgery at Oxford in 1937), was so shocked by the loss of this iconic war hero that he went on to make a major study of head injuries suffered by motorcycle despatch riders. This led directly to the invention and wide use of crash helmets by motorcyclists, which later became compulsory.

It is likely that T. E. Lawrence, in the years after the Arab Revolt, saw himself as having betrayed the Arab cause. He had seen the undignified scramble for the spoils of war at first hand and had been powerless in the face of European *realpolitik*. But whatever his own sense of failure, the legend of Lawrence as the most romantic hero of the Great War has an undiminished life of its own. He is arguably North Oxford's greatest son.

11 A War Memorial

THE PARISH WAR memorial stands next to St Margaret's Church at the corner of Kingston Road and St Margaret's Road. It was erected in 1919 to honour the members of the armed forces from the parish who had fallen in the First World War: 47 men, representing between them a cross-section of all those who died in the Great War. It is unusual for its time, in that the names of the dead are given without their military rank.

They were mostly in their teens and twenties, but two were forty years old. Twelve were Oxford undergraduates. Eleven lived in Hayfield Road, ten in the Woodstock Road, nine in Kingston Road, six in Chalfont Road. Almost every street in the parish lost at least one man; and, because most of the letter boxes have never been changed, it is not hard to imagine the postman in 1916 posting the dreaded telegram through that box.

In 1916 seventeen men from our parish died. Three of them were killed in action in France on the same day: 3 September 1916.

There were four pairs of brothers. Seven of the men were married and, of those, five had children. Forty served in the British Army, but two were in the Royal Flying Corps/RAF, and one each in the Indian, Canadian, and Australian armies. They came from all ranks: privates, NCOs, and officers. They mostly died in France and Belgium, but some met their end in Iraq, the Persian Gulf, Turkey, Egypt, and Israel. Twenty-one of them have no known grave.

Pte. ALBERT PHIPPS, Oxf. and
Bucks Lt. Infy., Heyfield-road.—
Died of wounds.

Albert Phipps

War Memorial 2007

Pte. P. H. PHIPPS, Hayfield-road,
Oxford, 1st Batt. O.B.L.I.—Accidentally drowned in Persian Gulf.

Percival Phipps

Percy Campbell

Sadly, it is too late to gather reminiscences of these men from those who loved them, but we have at least been able to document the salient facts of each man's life. These are the stories of five of them.

Arthur Morris (1899–1918)

ARTHUR MORRIS WAS the ninth child of Charles Morris and Ellen Louisa Peverell. Both his parents came from Bletchingdon, where Charles was a general labourer. They were married at the age of 22 in 1882. Ellen was to have 18 children, eleven of whom survived infancy. By 1884 they had moved to Oxford, and by 1898 were living at 74 Hayfield Road, where Arthur was born in the following year.

Arthur's mother died at the age of 47, around the time of his eighth birthday, but luckily there were several older sisters to take care of him. It appears that he was a sickly boy – his sister Elsie remembered that "our Arthur" always had to have the place by the fire, and the injunction to "save that last bit for Arthur" was often heard. Both his parents worried about his health. Arthur's father Charles continued to work as a corporation labourer and in 1911, when Arthur was 11, he still had eight of his children living with him.

In the First World War, Arthur Morris served as a Private in the 2nd Battn. Northamptonshire Regiment. Shortly before he went to the front, in March 1918, he was admitted to the Radcliffe Infirmary with appendicitis, which, in the days before antibiotics, was a grave illness, requiring a long convalescence after surgery. His eldest brother Charlie, himself serving at the Front, wrote after Arthur's death: *"It makes me nearly choke to think about the way he was treated for he was never fit for active service and it's a wonder he stuck it as well as he did ... I think everyone who knew him felt sorry he had to join up ... we all should be proud of a lad like him doing his bit without a lot of grumbling."*

On 8 April 1918 Arthur wrote to Elsie, *"Just a few lines to let you know I'm getting on alright out here. Sorry I did not write before. We had a nice voyage on the sea. It was very calm and it didn't take*

71

long to get here ..." Arthur arrived in time for the desperate Spring Offensive of March–July 1918, mounted by Ludendorff against the Allied armies on the Western Front. At that stage it seemed possible that Germany might finally prevail against the Allies.

Arthur had been in France for less than three weeks when he suffered a severe shrapnel wound in the abdomen. He died at a Casualty Clearing Station on the same day, 25 April 1918. His father was informed: "In spite of all that was done for your Son, he never rallied nor regained consciousness." He was twenty years old, one among 420,000 British soldiers who died in the Spring Offensive. He is remembered only on the St Margaret's War Memorial.

Arthur's two elder brothers Charlie and Frank both survived the war. Charlie wrote in May 1918: *"What a thing luck is, there's Frank been out all the time and not a scratch and Arthur (only) a few weeks. Frank has been doing something great by all accounts, but will he get the reward? Pleased to say I'm keeping in the pink, but shall be glad when it's over."* Frank had risked his own life to save that of another man, but never got the medal that Charlie thought he deserved.

Both brothers became greengrocers. Frank's shop was in North Parade, and Charlie's in Summertown Parade. Their sister Elsie and youngest brother William and his family lived on in Hayfield Road. Elsie, born in 1893, lived until 1979.

Herbert Gee (1877–1918)

HERBERT WAS BORN in Oxford in 1877, the fifth of seven children. At the time of the 1871 census his father, William Henry Gee, was a bookseller. He employed a porter and one apprentice and was living with his new wife and their house servant at Beef Lane, St Aldate's. Trade directories show that he then sold secondhand books at 28 High Street, Oxford. From 1879 to 1890 the family lived at 4, The Terrace, Park Town. The shop was demolished in the mid-1880s to make way for the extension of Brasenose College into the High. By

1889 Herbert's father had moved his shop across the road to 127 High Street, and the following year the family moved to 35 Southmoor Road. They were living there at the time of the 1891 census: Herbert, who attended the Oxford High School for Boys in George Street, was then a schoolboy of 13.

William Henry Gee's bookshop in the High Street closed down in about 1894, and at the time of the 1901 census he described himself as a political agent. Herbert himself was not at home on census night.

By the time of the 1911 census, Herbert's father was a widower. He had moved to 3 Southmoor Road, still in St Margaret's parish, a large house with eleven rooms, and the family had one servant. Of his seven children, only Lizzie, Alice, and Frederick were still at home. Herbert (33) was now a commercial traveller, selling typewriter accessories and living at 50 Fairmount Road, Brixton Hill, London, with his married brother Charles, who worked in a bookshop.

About a month after the census, on 4 May 1911, Herbert Gee emigrated to Australia: passenger lists show "H. Gee" (an adult single male, occupation "Traveller") sailing that day with the White Star Line on the *Medic* from Liverpool to Sydney. He took up farming at East Barron Atherton, Queensland.

On 1 April 1915 Herbert, then aged 37, enlisted in the 11th Australian Light Horse Regiment, Australian Imperial Force (AIF), "B" Squadron. He was appointed a Second Lieutenant and embarked with his squadron from Brisbane on board HMAT A30 *Borda* on 16 June 1915. He was sent to Gallipoli, where he was wounded on 3 September and again on 3 November 1915. He was mentioned twice in despatches and won the Military Cross on 28 December 1917 and Bar in April 1917.

When Australian soldiers were granted leave, they would go to either London or Paris, where barracks and lodgings were provided for them at nominal expense. It is therefore likely that it was our Herbert J. Gee who married Eleanor Glasow (born in Woolwich in 1885) in autumn 1916 in Lambeth. They had one child.

By 1918 Herbert John Gee was a Captain and fighting in Palestine. He and his men entered the railway station buildings in Semakh (a small town on the southern shore of Lake Tiberias); armed with bayonets, they destroyed or captured the whole German force (which was armed with machine-guns and grenades and much larger than the Australian one). He died in this action on 25 September 1918, aged 40, and is buried in the Haifa War cemetery.

Percival Phipps (1893–1915) and Albert Phipps (1898–1916)

PERCIVAL AND ALBERT were the two eldest sons of Henry Phipps and Sarah Harper, who had in all nine children. The census returns show how the lives of Henry and Sarah changed as they moved from country to town. In 1891 Henry was working as a hay binder (making hay bundles for winter feed) in Hook Norton, and Sarah was a domestic servant in Hertfordshire. They married later that year and by 1901 were living in Wolvercote. Henry was still a hay binder, but Sarah, with four young children, was a dressmaker, presumably working at home.

By 1907 the Phipps family, now with six children, had moved further into Oxford, to 26 Hayfield Road. By this time Henry was a furniture remover, but his eldest son Percival, now 18, had already joined the army. Albert, at 14, was working as an under-butler, probably at a college.

In the Great War Percival served as a Private in the 1st Battn. Oxon & Bucks Light Infantry. He was accidentally drowned in the Persian Gulf at the age of 21 on 5 April 1915 and is buried in the Basra War Cemetery, Iraq. Albert, like his brother, served as a Private in the 1st/4th Battn. Oxon & Bucks, but in a different theatre of war. He died of wounds in France at the age of 18 on 25 November 1916 and is buried at Rouen.

Percy Campbell (1894–1914)

PERCY, BORN ON 2 May 1894, lived at 25 St Margaret's Road, Oxford. He attended the Dragon School and Clifton College, where he "never cared very much for games". In 1913 he went up to Hertford College, Oxford, to study medicine. When war was declared in August 1914, Percy immediately joined up and was gazetted to the Wiltshire Regiment. On 24 August he went off to Weymouth for five weeks' training and on 5 October sailed for Flanders in a cattle boat. He wrote to his father: "*I expect we will all wish to be back as soon as we are out there. It will be such a hell.*" They stayed a few days in Ostend, where he bought chocolate for his men. He wrote home on 10 October: "*I have just been playing a few folksongs on the piano in the billet ... I don't like these cobbled roads at all, they make marching very hard.*"

On 13 October the Wiltshires arrived at Ypres and dug trenches along the Menin–Ypres road. On 20 October the First Battle of Ypres began. On the first three days the casualties were comparatively slight, but on 24 October the German heavy shells found the Wiltshire trenches, which were blasted out. "*The German infantry came on in thousands, and the last of my battalion charged with the bayonet*", reported Captain Comyns.

Percy's platoon held the extreme end of the Wiltshire line. It is said that he did all he could to cheer the spirits of his men. He rendered first aid to the wounded and shared his rations with the men. "*He cheered us with his jokes*", said one of his men. "*There was no braver man in the firing line.*" When the Wiltshires were ordered to retreat, he got the remnants of his platoon back to safety, and then set off back to the trenches, not knowing that by this time they were occupied by the enemy.

The regiment was now surrounded, but Percy could still have got away. However, "*he heard that Lieutenant Fowle was wounded on the road, and he asked me to go back with him. I tried to persuade him not to go, as it was certain death or capture, but he took no notice of me, and so we went back, but before we got within fifty yards of him your son was hit ...."* (Captain Macnamara).

Percy's body was buried where he fell, but he has no named grave. He was reported "missing" on 24 October 1914. He was 20 years old. His name is recorded on the Menin Gate. This is part of a poem he wrote as a schoolboy:

> *Sadness is not the property of death*
> *Why should we call death sad?*
> *... The mother gives her son*
> *The husband gives his wife to peace*
> *Knowing they meet when all shall cease*
> *They see it should be done*
> *Though it may grieve and hurt their heart.*

Our obligation to the past

THE WAR MEMORIAL itself is unusual. It is a calvary with a figure of Christ, two-thirds life-size, hanging on an oak cross. Behind the calvary is a semi-circular low limestone wall, on which there are bronze plates bearing the names of the 47 men. The wall carries four oak pillars, which support an ornate plaster semi-dome.

The figure of Christ was one of two hundred cast at Lucy's Engineering, the iron foundry in nearby Jericho. Each would have been intended for a war memorial. The whereabouts of the other 199 are not known, but the hunt for them would be an interesting challenge, which we hope that someone will take up. Our memorial was given a Grade II listing in September 2007, on the basis that "standing ... on the street corner it is an ever-present reminder of the servicemen's sacrifice".

Requests to local people for contributions to the War Memorial Appeal fund frequently meet with the response "I didn't know it was a war memorial". So, in an attempt to change local perceptions, a wreath-laying ceremony is now held on every Remembrance Sunday, attended by an increasing number of people. In 2009 the wreath was laid by Percy Campbell, the nephew of Percy Campbell who is commemorated on the Memorial.

A second common response is "I don't like the calvary." All we can say is that this is what the community chose in 1919. They could have decided on a more austere, less Catholic, memorial, but instead they elected to raise a flamboyant late-Victorian shrine to their war dead, which – like it or loathe it – has become a focal point for our community. The front page of the *Oxford Journal Illustrated* for 29 October 1919, below photos of the new war memorials at St Margaret's and Wolvercote, noted: "The cross is at present leading the way in the style of war memorials".

Sadly the century has taken its toll on a memorial that must have looked spectacular in 1919 with its Tempietto-like design and starry blue dome, but it was not made for an English climate and is now much dilapidated. Lucy's took down and sandblasted the cast-iron figure of Christ in 1999, and it has been repainted twice since to keep rust at bay, but the bulk of reconstruction remains to be done. The oak pillars and the semi-dome have been eroded by beetle and rot, and they now need to be replaced as a matter of urgency.

In 2010, our research into the histories of our 47 men has uncovered only five families who still keep alive the memory of their dead: those of Albert Colmer, Percy Campbell, Arthur Morris, Norman Smith, and the brothers Alexander and Cyril Wallace. So it falls to all of us, as inheritors of the community which bore their loss, to keep their memory alive.

Information about each man named on the memorial, and several photographs, can be found on our website at www.headington.org. uk/oxon/stmargaret. Stephanie Jenkins set up the website and cheerfully undertook the huge volume of research that has been necessary. We would be delighted if readers could provide any more information; and of course any contribution that you would like to make to the Appeal would be most welcome. Details of how to do this are given on the website and on the Appeal notice board next to the memorial.

Acknowledgements

OUR THANKS ARE due to Richard Webster for permission to use his original design; to Ralph Hall at Oxford Designers & Illustrators for his creative input, and to Peter Lawrence at ODI for valuable support and advice; to Revd Dr Andrew Bunch for his contributions to the text of chapters 4 and 6; and to all those who kindly gave us permission to use copyright photographs and drawings.

Every effort has been made to trace the owners of copyright material, in a few cases without success. If any copyright has been inadvertently infringed, we apologise and ask to be informed, so that amends may be made in any future edition. Copyright on the following illustrations is held by the individuals and organisations listed below:

Pages vi, 4, 8, and 70 (top left and bottom left): Images and Voices, Oxfordshire County Council
Pages 16, 56, and 58: Liz Wade
Page 26: St Margaret's Institute archives
Page 39: Polly Holbrook
Page 61: Alan Allport
Page 62: Caroline Jackson-Houlston
Page 70 (bottom right): The Campbell family
Page 82: Thomas Davies
Cover: Polly Holbrook (May Day ox), Images and Voices, Oxfordshire County Council (old Anchor Inn), Felicity Wood (child in Trap Grounds); all other images: Liz Wade

Sources and Bibliography

General

- *The Encyclopaedia of Oxford*, ed. C. and E. Hibbert (Macmillan, 1988).
- *North Oxford* by Tanis Hinchcliffe (Yale University Press, 1992).
- *The Victoria History of the County of Oxfordshire, Volume IV* (Oxford University Press, 1979).

Chapter 1: The Community at the Crossroads

- *Dissertation on the Antiquities of Oxford* by Leonard Hutten (1625).
- *Oxford Topography* by Hubert Hurst (1899).
- Minn Collection, Bodleian Library.

Chapter 2: The Anchor

- *The Life and Times of Anthony Wood, Antiquary, of Oxford, 1632-1695, Described by Himself,* edited by Andrew Clark (Oxford Historical Society, 1891–1900)
- *Jackson's Oxford Journal* and *The Oxford Times* (City Library archives).
- *Oxon Brews: The Story of Commercial Brewing in Oxfordshire* by Mike Brown (2004).

Chapter 3: Canal and Railway

- *The Oxford Canal* by Hugh J. Compton (David & Charles, 1976).
- *A Towpath Walk in Oxford* by Mark Davies and Catherine Robinson (Towpath Press, 2001).
- *Ramlin Rose: The Boatwoman's Story* by Sheila Stewart (Oxford University Press, 1993).

- Author's interviews with Mrs Sylvia Johnson, 1999; Jack and Rose Skinner, 2000.

Chapter 4: St Margaret's Church
- www.stmargaretsoxford.org/thechurch/270/the-history-of-the-parish.
- Information from John Davies.

Chapter 5: St Margaret's Institute
- Copies of St Margaret's parish magazine from 1901, 1902, 1906, 1928, and 1929 (Bodleian Library).
- Archives of *The Oxford Times,* June 1945.
- Notes written by Miss Eleanor Wood and Miss Jinner Snodgrass (both now deceased).
- Interviews and correspondence with local residents and organisers of activities: Lisa Astley-Sparke, Peggy Bainbridge (now deceased), Rev. Dr. Andrew Bunch, Romy Briant, Susan Coleman, Nancy Drucker, Graham Hooper, Helen Hunter, Martin Koretz, Dorothy Metcalf, Lisa Morgan, Sir Derek Morris, Joyce Newman, Ben Simpson, Sandra Steeples, Stuart Skyte, Joey Slessor, Dr Ann Taylor, Barbara Wanklyn, Bryan Wardley, Roger Wicksteed.
- *Hayfield Road: Nine Hundred Years of an Oxford Neighbourhood* by Catherine Robinson and Elspeth Buxton (1993).
- Archives of St Margaret's Institute.

Chapter 6: Phil & Jim School
- *The Changing Face of North Oxford, Book II,* by Ann Spokes Symonds.
- "Ss. Philip and James Schools from 1873 to 1979", by Karen Hewitt.
- Information from Tom Appleton and Bridget Thompson.

Chapter 7: Hayfield Road
- The national Census for 1841, 1851, 1861, 1881, and 1891.
- *Jackson's Oxford Journal* and *The Oxford Times* (City Library archives).
- St Margaret's parish magazines (stored in the Bodleian Library).
- Documents from the archives of St John's College.

- *Hayfield Road: Nine Hundred Years Of An Oxford Neighbourhood* (Catherine Robinson and Elspeth Buxton, 1993).
- Author's interviews in 1993 with Mr Bob Ayres, Mrs Mary Giles, Miss Florrie Goddard, Mrs Jessie Harding, Miss Molly Harris, Mrs Nora Surman, and Mrs Doris Thicke (all now deceased).

Chapter 8: Aladdin and Bunter's

- *Jackson's Oxford Journal* (City Library archives).
- Kelly's Trade Directory, various years.
- Author's interviews in 2010 with Kelvin Chambers, Gill Chambers, Peter Saini and Peter Lawrence.

Chapter 9: The Trap Grounds

Website of the Friends of the Trap Grounds: www.trap-grounds.org.uk.

Chapter 10: Lawrence of Arabia

- "The first modern celebrity" is a quotation from "Lawrence of Arabia rides again" by Philip Knightley, *Sunday Times*, 5 October 2005.
- "All men dream ...": from Lawrence's *Seven Pillars of Wisdom*.
- "The uncrowned King of Arabia" was said of Lawrence by Ronald Storrs, Governor of Jerusalem, to Lowell Thomas.
- *Lawrence, the Uncrowned King of Arabia* by Michael Asher, 1998.
- "Lawrence of Arabia, Sir Hugh Cairns and the origin of motorcycle helmets" by Maartens, Wills, and Adams in *Neurosurgery* 2002 Jan.50 (1): 176–9.

Chapter 11: The War Memorial

- The memorial website, www.headington.org.uk/oxon/stmargaret, for biographies and analysis, compiled by Stephanie Jenkins.
- "Memoir: Percy Campbell", printed for private circulation and kindly lent to the author by Jim Campbell.
- Interviews with Madelaine Morris and Jim Campbell.

The Community at the Crossroads: A Map

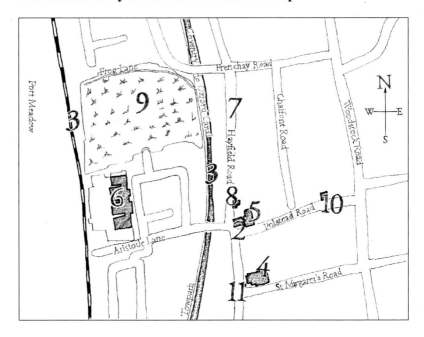

Places in the text are identified by chapter numbers:

Lightning Source UK Ltd.
Milton Keynes UK
UKOW041852281012

201322UK00001B/11/P